HOW TO GET A
Glamour
Job

HOW TO GET A
Glamour Job

 by Laura Schwartz and Marcia Dorfman

NYT

Quadrangle / The New York Times Book Co.

Library of Congress Cataloging in Publication Data

Schwartz, Laura.
    How to get a glamour job.

    1. Vocational guidance for women.   I. Dorfman, Marcia, joint author.   II. Title.
HD6058.S423   1977   650′.14′024042   76-50816
ISBN 0-8129-0671-3

For Gerry and Irwin and Spsina

1957929

❧ Contents

Foreword

Knowing how to get a job is an acquired skill, like driving a car. It takes practice and know-how, but it can be learned. The prospect of looking for a job may seem overwhelming, but it needn't be. What we hope to do in this book is help you overcome the obstacles in your path to successful job hunting by explaining how to go about it, in everyday language.

Obviously, there's no magic we can perform to land you the job of your dreams. Only Merlin can do that. What we can do is to provide some insight into the workings of the professional world and offer some well-tested survival techniques to prevent you from making some of the same mistakes we did. If we knew then, back when we started our careers, what we know now, we would have saved ourselves a lot of wasted time and frustration. We want to spare you that. There's an old saw that says people can only learn from personal experience; we don't believe it. Neither do scores of professional women we talked to who were eager to share their thoughts and advice on the subject of job hunting and careers.

We've chosen the glamour industries as the framework for this book for a variety of reasons. First of all, like so many other people, we are fascinated by the entertainment, communications, and fashion businesses. Secondly, women have traditionally been able to establish fine careers in these fields when other areas were more than reluctant to include them. Despite the fact that inequities still exist, conditions *are* getting better. Finally, we believe that if you're going to expend the considerable effort entailed in building a career, you might as well enjoy some of the benefits that are part of the glamour business. Not the least of which is that even beginning jobs are unusually appealing. However, no matter which specific career you ultimately select, you're going to have to start at the bottom and work your way to the top. One way or another, all of us have to pay our dues. The road to success in the glamour world, however, is traveled along a more scenic route.

We think this book will be useful for anyone looking for a job, male or female, in any industry. But we are women writing, principally, for women: girls graduating from school, career women who want to switch fields, women who are not working now but want to be. This book will tell you how to get a job, successfully, but our emphasis is on careers, not jobs. And there's a world of difference. A job can keep you busy nine-to-five, pay you a salary, and not necessarily lead anywhere. A career is a life's work and, as such, must be nurtured appropriately. Step by step, carefully. We're going to help you evaluate a job from that point of view. All too often, jobs don't fully utilize our abilities or fully realize our potential. The right career does. It's no wonder then that more and more women, regardless of age or previous experience, are seeking work that is more than a time filler.

In researching this book, we did all our interviews "off the record." We found that people were far more willing to tell us the inside story, the unvarnished truth, if we assured them they wouldn't be identified. What we were after was the honest, gut-level information only a best friend would tell you, and, quite naturally, people hold back if they're going to be quoted. We chose to use pseudonyms rather than get half the truth or jeopardize anyone's career.

How to Get a Glamour Job will help you learn how to assess the kind of career that's right for you, with suggestions as to how to go about getting into it. You're willing to give up the most precious thing you have, time. In exchange, you're entitled to derive some measure of gratification, remuneration, or whatever will bring you the most pleasure. We think the glamour industries offer more opportunities to achieve what you want, and more fun while you're working toward it, than most other businesses. People who get ahead in a career work very hard, and have to have a certain amount of luck. We can't control the vicissitudes of Dame Fortune, but we can help you nudge her a little, or at least help you tilt the odds in your favor.

HOW TO GET A
Glamour Job

)

ONE

❧ *What's So Glamorous?*

"There's no such thing as a glamour job," Diane Von Furstenberg insisted in a recent television interview. The camera caught her as she stepped from a chauffeur-driven Mercedes-Benz after a two-day promotion trip to Las Vegas. There she was, all twenty-nine years of her, standing in front of the office building which headquarters her multimillion-dollar organization. Diane's sultry good looks personify glamour. She's the perfect model for her body-clinging, slinky designs. In fact, her name is synonymous with a whole way of dressing. The Von Furstenberg imprint can be found not only on clothes, but on cosmetics, perfume, accessories, sunglasses, and a posh Madison Avenue boutique, as well. In an average day, **Diane** is involved with designing, production, advertising, and meetings with business associates, the press, and her many customers. She flies across the Atlantic as casually as most people cross the street. And when her work day is over, she moves on to a social life that would be a full-time job in itself for a woman with less energy.

"You see," Diane continued, "the more glamorous a job looks from the outside, the harder the work usually is."

True enough, but whoever said that hard work can't be glamorous? Dazzling, head-spinning glamour comes with success, and success comes from hard work. The women we've met with the most exciting careers all work incredibly hard, but they're constantly stimulated, never bored. It's one of the reasons they love their jobs. Of course, there are routine aspects to any job; nobody's denying that. Even movie stars— who epitomize glamour in our culture—have to get up at the crack of dawn to get to the studio in time to be made up and costumed for a nine A.M. shooting. Then they cool their heels, waiting for lights, camera, and sound equipment to be adjusted properly. They speak a few lines, then wait again for the whole process to be repeated. It's slow, sometimes tedious, work. Yet which of us hasn't fantasized about being a glamorous movie star?

In reality, every career has its moments of frustration or tedium; it's marvelous if there can be exciting highs to offset them. Let's face it, what could be more glamorous than attending the Paris couture collections to see which designs *you* think will be most influential? Or rescuing a manuscript from obscurity because *you* see the special, best-seller qualities in it? Or writing the words which transform an unknown product into a national craze? These things may be the result of very hard work but it's gratifying, not to mention great fun.

Success is glamorous, and the life-style that goes with it in the glamour world has to be seen to be believed. It's great to be at the top of any profession, but the glamour industries are devoted to style—and life at the top positively glitters. Life on the way up isn't hard to take, either, but the glamour industries are like no other. Since Diane Von Furstenberg is absolutely right about the hard work, our thesis is that as long as you have to break your tail, you might as well choose a career that offers a little magic along with it. Glamour "benefits," happily, are not just the exclusive property of the precious few whose names are household words; they're enjoyed by thousands of people who work in the entertainment, fashion, and communications fields. These are businesses which deal with refinements, not the necessities of life, and concern themselves with such subtleties as style and taste. That's really what the glamour world is all about: tastemaking and trend-setting.

One secret of success in the glamour business is to be the first to sense a trend, spot a new talent, or rediscover an old art form. Very few of us are born with this talent. The tendency may be there, but it requires nurturing and experience to perfect. It takes constant exposure to everything that's new or artistic or exciting, and you have to keep up with what's happening. The glamour industries are so closely interrelated that it's important to be conversant with the doings in each of them, not just your own particular end of the business. Today's editor may well be tomorrow's author and next year's TV personality. If you're in the business of making movies, you'd better be aware of what's being published, because many of today's best-sellers began as screenplays, and vice-versa. The fashion world frequently derives its inspiration from the theater, or films, or the arts; and the reverse is often true as well. Movies, broadcasting, publishing, advertising, public relations, beauty, and fashion—these are the golden seven. As a result, the glamour world flourishes in its social life, combining business and pleasure. There are screenings, art openings, theater benefits, parties to introduce authors or launch new designers. There are intimate dinners where who's talking to whom about what converts gossip into tomorrow's news.

The need to be a part of everything that's going on results in life at a hectic clip. Glamour people do a lot of traveling. That's how the phrase "jet set" was born. Lots of the jet-set insiders are socialites, yes, but many of these "beautiful people" (as *Women's Wear Daily* refers to them) are hard-working, glamour-world denizens. The social columns are filled with their names: Estée Lauder, Mary Wells Lawrence, Geraldine Stutz, Sue Mengers, the list could go on and on. These women weren't born with silver spoons in their mouths. They're "items" because of their considerable business achievements. They all started at the bottom and worked their way to larger-than-life successes. So can you. That's part of the glamour; if you've got what it takes, you too can become a big, big winner.

Even moderate success in the glamour world brings with it special niceties. A ready-to-wear buyer at a

large department store told us, "I'm sure no one outside the business knows my name. I'm certainly not
recognized on the street, and I seriously doubt anyone
would say I lead a glamorous life. But when I walk
through the lobby of the Ritz in Paris, and the con-
cierge falls all over himself welcoming me, I realize I
must be getting up there. My plane was three hours
late on my last buying trip to Paris. Would you believe
the hotel maid was waiting for me to help me unpack
and get settled? And the management had filled my
suite with exquisite apricot-colored roses. They really
rolled out the red carpet for me. Sometimes it's hard to
remember that I'm the same girl who felt so deprived
because I had to go to work instead of college. I
haven't done badly for someone with only a high
school diploma."

Not everyone with a glamour job, as Diane Von
Furstenberg indicated, considers what they do for a
living as glamorous. Take Ellen, for instance. She
works for a film production house, specializing in TV
commercials. Ellen's the person who gets everything
together and ready for a "shoot." This might mean
flying to Spain—where production is cheaper—two
weeks ahead of the director and crew, to scout locations, hire local technicians, cast the extras, insure
that accommodations are acceptable, and so on.
Sounds marvelous doesn't it? Well, Ellen laughed
when we asked for an interview.

"Glamorous? Me? You must be kidding! What's so
glamorous about trying to negotiate for the rental of
tape equipment in Japanese?"

"It sounds better to us," we pointed out, "than trying to rent the same equipment in English on West 27th Street."

"I guess so. I love to travel and I do get to do a lot of it. I'm always off to someplace new, hunting up some strange thing or other. Like finding a place in Australia that looks like the South American jungle, or trying to cast a perfect monkey for a particularly complicated commercial."

"Your job sure sounds like fun to us," we said.

"I guess what I do is kind of special, when you think about it," Ellen admitted. "I adore it. It just never occurred to me that anyone would think of it as a glamour job. I suppose it really is. It's no everyday, run-of-the-mill job, that's for sure."

Hardly. How many people do you get to meet who can cast a cute monkey? So it all depends on your point of view. The glamour jobs we'll discuss in the following pages are as different as the women who hold them. Ellen's job is as far from a buyer's job as any two can be, yet both of them seem glamorous to us. Maybe you disagree. Glamour is such a subtle concept, it has different nuances for different people. We've discovered that glamour is in the eye of the beholder. Most people don't seem to consider their own jobs glamorous. Or, as one woman phrased it, "a glamour job is your job, not mine." It's funny, but even the most successful women turned out to be intrigued by their friends' jobs. When we indicated that *we* thought *their* jobs were just as exciting, they always seemed surprised. Still, no matter what your personal definition of glamour may be, you'll find plenty of job opportunities that will fulfill your individual conception. And no matter which of our suggested career paths you take, you're going to be on the receiving end of some of the glamour "benefits" we'll be talking about.

People in the glamour industries seem to do things in a special way. Even the most humdrum practices are handled imaginatively. A friend of ours, who's a creative director at a New York advertising agency, told us about a winter weekend business meeting we think typifies glamour style. Morale at the agency was low, and management thought that a top echelon retreat was needed to review overall agency direction. The problem was they didn't want to plan a meeting the executives would resent having to attend. Here's what they did:

Thirty executives, and their husbands and wives, were invited to a "think tank" weekend, destination unknown. A short questionnaire was sent to each executive, asking several somewhat-odd questions, such as "What do you drink before dinner?" Everyone was told to pack beach-wear and a passport. Friday morning, limousines were dispatched to collect the group and take them to the airport. Everyone's luggage was labelled with specially designed leather tags with the individual's name embossed in gold. After boarding a privately chartered jet, the group was served a superb meal and champagne. The plane landed in Acapulco. The group was driven to a fabulous resort, where each couple had a private cottage with its own swimming pool. Each cottage was filled with fresh flowers, each kitchen stocked with the individual preferences itemized on the questionnaire. The best part of all, we're told, was that any socializing was optional. They were free to join the group's planned excursions and dinners, or go off on their own. As our friend said, "Company meetings can be deadly anyway, but the worst of it is always the endless social garbage. You go home feeling as if you've spent a month with those same faces. Here, we all got a free weekend we could really enjoy. We had three conferences that weekend and, believe it or not, they were actually productive. What's more, morale at the office soared." We believe it.

As we said, there's an emphasis placed on style in the glamour industries that makes working in them, well, glamorous. After a while, people begin to take this rather unusual lifestyle for granted. It's human nature. All of us get used to the good life very easily. We had a conversation at lunch recently which brought this point home to us quite clearly. We were waiting for our friend, Celine, the taste maven,* at Orsini's, a well-known glamour hangout in the West Fifties. It's a marvelous, small restaurant with lovely marble tables and a jungle of greenery all but obliterating the front windows. Celine came dashing in, dressed in black from head to toe, with sunglasses

---

* If you're planning a career in any of the glamour industries, you'd better know now that a *maven* is an expert, a connoisseur.

perched atop her tousled blond hair. Somehow, every time we see her she looks better than the last time. She must be well over forty by now, but her looks are ageless and flawless. We considered hating her, but decided against it. She greeted us with a wave of her hand (nails manicured impeccably, of course) and proceeded to tell us her problems.

"Everything is so mixed up. I was supposed to fly to Bali next week to shoot the resort clothes for the magazine, but the hairdresser is unavailable then. The photographer who was going to Barbados to do the holiday issue refuses to go unless the magazine sends me to supervise. But I have to be in Florence for the Italian ready-to-wear collections. It's impossible."

We tried to commiserate. Celine did have problems that required complicated juggling to solve, but all of a sudden the three of us dissolved in laughter. "Listen to me complain," Celine said. "Everyone's business problems should be so terrible."

How right she is. You're going to be faced with business problems of one sort or other, no matter what job you have. You're going to have to cope with all kinds of complications in any career. You might as well have the troubles of the glamour world. It may be tough to juggle Bali, Barbados, and Florence, but who'd object to a little juggling to get to see those places? It's a matter of making choices. Some problems are better to have than others, and some jobs are more fun to have than others. In the scheme of the world, we'd rather enjoy ourselves than not. Given the choice, we opt for careers that will help us grow intellectually, stimulate our minds, and excite our imaginations. Any career is a serious commitment in time and energy. You have to decide what you want to get in exchange.

TWO

ᴥ *Getting Started*

Okay, let's get started. People seem to spend an inordinate amount of time just spinning their wheels, accomplishing little. Because the prospect of looking for a job can be so overwhelming, it's often terribly hard to decide where to begin. We make lists and talk about "getting our act together," but, in fact, we wind up noplace. Most of us are torn between what we think we *should* do and what we *want* to do (the old guilt thing rears its ubiquitous head). It's a vicious cycle. The more we stew, the less we do; the more we feel we're accomplishing something, the better we feel, the more we do. Of course, there are the admirable self-starters among us, but they're probably off-and-running by now anyway. So, we're going to suggest some very simple organizing mechanisms to help you get moving. Believe us, they work.

For openers, you might read this book with a pad and pencil in hand. That way, you can keep track of ideas and suggestions particularly pertinent to you. Don't rely on your memory. That's rule one. Life is too busy, too filled with distractions to remember everything. We've found that a spiral notebook is handy for keeping random thoughts and notes in one readily available place—and prevents the inevitable aggravation of looking for loose pieces of paper here and there.

You should also start a "Job Hunting" file. Get a 5 × 8 file box with index cards, and file potential employers and personnel agencies alphabetically. Note everything that pertains to that company or agency on its card: conversations, miscellaneous information, names of people, and so on. Don't dismiss this as the ramblings of compulsive, fanatic organizers. Trust us, and do it. Careers are for life and job hunting is a part of career building. The job you're hoping to find now is just the first step. Because it's the first, things that seem cataclysmic today, things you'd swear you'll never forget, *will* fade in importance eventually, and be forgotten. You just won't be able to remember forever when you met whom and under what circumstances. Whether Mr. X said to call in the summer when things are quiet, or whether his company is bedlam in the summer, and it's better to call him in the fall.

Looking for a job, if you do it properly, involves as many people and companies as you can handle. It makes sense to keep them all straight. By the same token, a good career involves keeping up with every worthwhile contact you encounter. (And it's been our experience that we just never can remember everything we wish we could without a little help.) Case in point: a college graduate of our acquaintance was eager for a job, any kind of job, on a famous fashion magazine. She went to every magazine that would see her, including her first choice. The editor there told her, "Look, dear, make your mistakes elsewhere and then come back to see me." Well, our friend found a job on another magazine and did very nicely. But when the time came to go back to her favorite, she couldn't remember the name of the woman to see. Unbelievable? Not at all. Too many years, too many people, too many new experiences had intervened.

ASSESS YOURSELF

All right, we'll assume we've sold you on the idea of a card file for prospective employers and you are now sitting, pad in hand, reading this book. Now is the time for some serious, searingly honest soul-searching. *Know thyself* is the name of the game. Everything you do after this depends on how honest you are with yourself at this point. You're on the threshold of a critical period in your life because career decisions are life decisions. No matter what your personal values and priorities, if you have a career, it will be one of the major factors in your life. You may place other things above it, but your job will most certainly be one of the critical components in your day-to-day happiness. Therefore, the better suited you and your job are to each other, the greater your chances for success.

There's often a big difference between who you are and who others want you to be. So, who are you? What are your strengths? What are your weaknesses? List both. Some of us are born knowing what we want to do; others discover something along the way. If you want to be a writer, start there. There are myriad writing opportunities in all the glamour industries. Artists, mathematicians, and others with technical skills and training also fall into this "I know what I can do" category. But what about someone with no obvious talent? That person might start with what are considered to be weaknesses: hates routine and steady hours, for example. The glamour industries are full of crazy-hour jobs where nothing is the same from one day to the next. (That's part of the glamour, by the way: the variety.) The girl who would be perfect starting as a nine-to-five secretary to an account executive might hate being a go-fer for a photographer, shooting a TV commercial at midnight. And vice versa. Different strokes, as they say, for different folks.

Another key question: What do you like to do? This is not at all the same as "what do you do well?" because many of us are good at things we don't particularly love. Ask yourself the reverse, also. What do you hate to do? Here again, list things in every area of your life. Do you like to travel? Or do you feel uncomfortable in new places? Do you hate parties? Love them? How about people? Do you enjoy being a leader? Or are you ill-at-ease in the spotlight? Do you hunger for The Big City? Or prefer small-town living? How do you feel about sports? clothes? food? New

York? Write down as many likes and dislikes as you can about yourself.

What you are doing by answering these questions is creating guidelines for yourself. If you dislike New York and crowds but adore clothes, the fashion world of Seventh Avenue isn't for you. There are other important fashion centers to investigate instead; Dallas, Los Angeles, not to mention the thousands of department stores and boutiques in every city in the country. You see what we mean. How ambitious are you? Before you begin to look for a job, you should have a pretty fair idea of where you want that job to lead. But before you come to that decision, you have to ask yourself what your own personal priorities are, how you see your career fitting into your everyday life. It might prove helpful to divide your life into areas: career, family, social life, leisure, special interests (hobbies, athletics, whatever). Add anything else relevant to you. Exactly how important is each of these areas to you? It's not easy to project how you're going to feel later on, but you can try. For instance, you may feel strongly that women should be as free as men to pursue careers, and be eager for a no-holds-barred career for yourself. This can cause conflicts in your personal life. Remember to avoid confusing what others want for you and from you with what you want for yourself. It's *you* who's going to go to work every day, not your mother or husband or child. How much time are *you* willing to give? How much aggravation will *you* put up with? Are you looking for something that's relatively pleasant from the outset? Or are you willing to put in some time that's pretty tough-going, if the future stakes are high enough?

And speaking of high stakes, how important is money to you? Our career fantasies usually involve several of the key "glamour" elements in various combinations: money, power, important people, fame, fun, excitement, intrigue. What matters to you the most? In the private screening room of your mind, how do you project your career? Are you the world-famous author? Or the author's agent? Are you an industry queen? Or the power behind the throne? Does fame interest you? Or would you prefer fortune and anonymity?

As we said, it's hard to nail these things down, but you can pretty well gauge your inclinations. Ambition is a funny thing. It grows with success. So you'll discover more about your personal ambitions *after* you've worked for a while. Just the same, it's worth thinking about here because it might help you decide whether to move to another city or not, whether to pursue one career or another. Of course, the decisions you'll be making are first-job decisions and, obviously, subject to change (as you change) and get working experience. So don't be put off by what may seem to be permanent, signed-in-blood choices. You have to start someplace, be an inexperienced beginner in some job. You'll get the feel of what you want and where you're going sooner than you think. More people than you can believe find that they have commercial talents they never dreamed of. And not just the traditional winners either. Recently, we spoke to a young woman who moved to New York right after college, dreaming of a career, any career, in television. Through a friend of a friend, she found a job answering a TV star's fan mail. "I stuck my finger into every pie I could," she said. "I worked on anything and everything that came into the office. I didn't care how late I worked or how menial the chore was. I'd gotten my foot in the door and I wanted to make sure they'd want to keep me around." They not only wanted to keep her around, but she worked her way into a super career as an associate director on the Jack Paar and David Frost shows. Today, she's the associate director on one of daytime TV's top-rated shows. Not bad for someone who wasn't sure where she was headed.

The thing to keep in mind is that you want to be open to the opportunities that come your way, to see how you act and react in a professional situation. Don't be timid about your ambitions, whatever they are, high or more down-to-earth. The associate director we mentioned was persistent and hardworking until she achieved her goal. It's equally appropriate to aim skyward—without having delusions of grandeur or a lust for power—as it is not to want a totally consuming career, and a more traditional home life. The truth of it is, you only live once; so you might as well be happy. Too often our Puritan ethic of "it's not work if it's fun" colors our decisions. Well, we're against that. Every job in the world has what medical interns call "scut" work; you know, the trivial routine everyone hates to do. Okay, that's got to be done. But within that framework, you certainly should be happy, enjoy what you're doing. And if *fun* is a dirty word, so be it. Be honest with yourself about what you really want. We promise that your ambitions and abilities will adjust to each other as you go along in your career.

Should the Mountain Go to Mohammed?

Do you have to move if you want a glamour career? Without meaning to straddle the fence, the answer is maybe. It depends on your priorities. You don't necessarily have to move anywhere. Department stores, boutiques, local TV, radio stations, ad agencies and so on are located just about everyplace within commuting distance. So you can stay put. There's nothing sadder than a small-town personality adrift in the big city. The point is: are you a small-town personality? Native New Yorkers are scarcer than hen's teeth in the glamour industries. They're crammed with people from every section of the country, from every hamlet you never heard of. Admittedly, it takes time to adjust to the pace, the crowds, the prices, but millions do it. How do you feel about it?

Some very successful people "make it" in New York and decide, after a while, that a slower pace, a less hectic lifestyle is more to their liking. So, they move elsewhere. *TV Guide* had an interesting article recently about several TV news reporters who left their big-city network positions to go back to local stations.

The reporters in question seemed to feel they could make more money in more important positions, with more air time, *and* have better home lives, too, outside of New York City. Or maybe it was the big-fish-in-a-little-pond syndrome. Whatever it was, despite the loss of status (because it's pretty impressive to be working for one of the big networks) and the absence of national exposure (which can be pretty "heady"), off they went. Connie Chung, former CBS news correspondent, moved to Los Angeles's KNXT, the CBS-owned-and-operated station. Of course, L.A. is hardly a small town, but it's not New York, either. The quality of life is becoming a determining factor for lots of people. Not just you. There are industries, like broadcasting for instance, where you might do better to start *out* of New York anyway.

Having said all this, and all things being equal, if you really want a glamour career and if your primary interest is your career, New York is where it's at. If only by sheer numbers. There are just more jobs to be had there, and more opportunities in a greater number of fields. The other big cities—Los Angeles, Chicago, Washington, San Francisco, Dallas and the like—are good; they're just not first. The other cities have much to offer in addition to more sky to look at and less-congested conditions. But New York has it all: TV, fashion, advertising, publishing, even movies (although L.A. is obviously the place for that!).

We realize that not everyone is in a position to pick up and move. Some people just don't want to; others may have family ties; there are a number of reasons.

A little further on, we'll make some suggestions for those of you who prefer to stay near where you are. But for everyone else, from those of you still in school to anyone living in but hating Smalltown, U.S.A., go to New York. We're not going to tell you to ignore all the bad things you've heard. We're going to suggest that the good things far outweigh the negatives. There are very few places left in the world with ideal living conditions, including New York. But there are fewer places in the world that are more exciting, challenging, inspiring. Sure, it's crowded and dirty; yes, the tempo can be frenetic. But when you're talking glamour geography, New York is Mecca. And no wonder. Anything goes and everything is available. Whatever your interest—the arts, food, shopping, sports—New York has it in spades. As far as your career is concerned, of course, New York is the major leagues. So if you've assessed yourself as a potential first stringer, don't head for the hills.

It's not as frightening a thought as you might think. There are temporary agencies for work to tide you over until you find a job. We'll discuss them in some detail in Chapter 3, "Down to Brass Tacks." There are special agencies whose business is to find compatible roommates, so you won't have to live alone or pay an astronomical rent by yourself. You'll meet dozens of people job-hunting, at churches, at the famous 92nd Street "Y" (one of New York's greatest cultural havens), at the local D'Agostino's. New York is friendlier than its reputation. If you think about it, you probably know someone living in New York already. Call them.

New Yorkers are used to hearing from out-of-towners and are usually more than happy to help.

If you just can't face New York at this point, the other big cities offer almost as many career opportunities. Every city has a major retail store; check their training programs. The fashion industry has big centers in Dallas, Miami, California; investigate, maybe there's something near you. Publishing is far less centralized than it used to be. Some of the biggest winners in recent years have emerged from heretofore unknown houses; look into them. Even small towns have local newspapers and radio stations. One of the best ways to break into television would be to take a job in a city with a network owned-and-operated station. Even if you work for a rival station, you'll get terrific experience and the chance to be seen by someone at the network station. They don't only watch their own channel!

Edwin Newman, noted NBC newscaster, interviewer, and writer, told us that it's "paid experience that counts." So, if you can cut your baby teeth on a local station, you'll be that much more hireable when you're looking for a better job at a bigger station. Most cities have ad agencies servicing local merchants. With more and more companies moving out of the larger cities, these local shops are acquiring some pretty impressive accounts. The big companies based in your hometown must have departments that handle their advertising, public relations, and the like. Go talk to them.

We don't mean to equivocate. Where you choose

to live is a very personal decision, although not necessarily a permanent one. If you start your career in a
large city and find out that big city living isn't for you;
don't worry. Big time experience is very marketable.
If you're afraid of making a dramatic move to the big
city now and want to start your career where you feel
more at home, fine. You can try a big city later on.
Small town experience is not as easily transferable, but
any experience is a plus. Many buyers, broadcasters,
newspaper people, you name it, have started out in
their home towns and moved up and out. As we said
earlier, do what makes you happy.

PACKAGE YOURSELF

Who says you can't judge a book by its cover?
Or, at least, its fly leaf? People do, every day. It's
often the outer wrapping that makes the sale, especially in the glamour industries, where the price of
anything goes up 50 percent the minute you add a designer's name to it. In a job-hunting situation, you've
got to sell yourself. An employer is buying a package:
you. You have skills, a personality, and an appearance;
you need all three in the right combination to get the
job. We're going to discuss all aspects of your total
"package," but we're going to start on the outside, on
the surface.

First impressions are, by their very nature, formed
in a flash from superficial details. Your appearance

and mannerisms are *your* outer package; they say something about you to strangers. What you have to analyze is whether your appearance is saying what you'd like it to say. How you look and present yourself has a profound effect on a prospective employer's reaction to you as a job candidate. It would be foolish, therefore, to ignore what can become an important, additional asset.

Spend some time examining your appearance. Do you look like a working woman? Or are you still locked into your student (or housewife or mother) garb? Pretend you're an actress trying out for the role of whatever job your interview is for. How you look is an indication of how you perceive yourself. If you think of yourself as a student, you'll look like one. If you want to look like a career woman, you'll have to begin to think like one.

What does a career woman look like? Better still, what does a successful career woman look like? Neat and well-groomed, always. Beyond that, she understands how to dress appropriately. Think actress again. How would central casting describe the woman needed for the part? Never go to an interview for a secretarial position dressed like the boss. It's not a smart thing to do because nobody hires anyone who looks like they'd be a threat. Save your finery for your social life. You're a beginner, or close to it, so look like one. Play it safe by wearing a shirt and skirt or a simple dress. Leave your blue jeans at home, even if you know that others wear them to that particular office. Once you have the job, you can dress like everyone else. For interviews, we recommend the safest thing in your closet. Don't wear your "best" dress, either. Employers have told us they have turned down people because they look like they don't need the job. One buyer who was looking for an assistant told us, "I took one look at this woman, dressed in a chic ultra-suede shirtdress, and crossed her right off the list. She was so obviously well-to-do. It was probably unfair of me, but her dress cost almost as much as she'd earn here in a month. I just couldn't picture her doing some of the more mundane chores I expect from my assistant." We don't really blame the buyer. It can be uncomfortable to ask someone to do menial tasks for you, even if it's part of the job. Why make yourself more uncomfortable by hiring someone who intensifies that feeling?

Grooming is unquestionably more important than what you wear. One executive told us that she looks at someone's hands first. To her, nail biters are high-strung and nervous, so she avoids them. Obviously, you won't appear capable and efficient if you're disheveled, so be sure your clothes are clean and pressed. Get your hair out of your face. Try not to fidget. This is as good a time as any to try to break any distracting mannerisms. Hair twirlers, finger drummers, and knee shakers drive most people up the wall. Do yourself a favor, and work on eliminating nervous habits.

These are the basics. As you move up in your career, keep your appearance in mind. You should change your "look" slightly, as your status improves. It should be an evolutionary process, however, not a revolution. As you assume more responsibility and earn more money, that growth and maturity should be reflected in your personal style. The glamour industries are very style conscious; you'll notice that once you start working. Make note of how the people who get ahead look and act. The most successful people have a self-confident aura about them, including the visual impression they give. Nurture your sense of individual style. People don't make it on packaging alone, but it can only help you.

Our original intention was to end this section here, but many people have pressed us for further details on the subject. "How do you trade-up your wardrobe?" we were asked. "My salary is small. Where should I spend what little extra I have?" The first thing to do is to get into shape. If you feel well, you'll look well. Most of us could stand to lose a few pounds; do it. That accomplishment is enough to give you a feeling of self-confidence. We can't prove it, but we're willing to bet that if anyone did a study on the relationship between being thin and being successful in the glamour industries, they'd find a depressing correlation. Next, get a good haircut. Well-styled hair goes with everything in your closet. It can make a big difference in how you look, how you feel about yourself. As for make-up, less is more. One thing that surprised us about the women in the beauty business is that they look so *un*made-up. Undoubtedly, these women were using lots of cosmetic products, but they were applied so skillfully you couldn't tell. Unless you're an expert, go easy.

In terms of your wardrobe, one good outfit is worth a dozen things that are just okay. You're not going to be judged on how large a wardrobe you have. No one will notice how often you wear something. Other than one special dress, buy basics. If you have a few, very simple things, you can invest your money in good accessories. That will do more for your total look than an extra sweater. Buying clothes in one color family can also stretch your dollars, because one set of accessories will do. As you get more affluent, add another color range. By all means read the fashion magazines. They're full of hints on how to update the look of what you already own.

Make no mistake about it, appearance is just as important for men as women. The specifics may differ, but successful men tend to be just as polished, just as fashionable as successful women. And we don't only mean men in the glamour industries; politicians, lawyers, bankers, men in all businesses have become much more concerned with improving their appearance. As we said, the image you have of yourself affects the image you project for others to see. Men are catching on, and it's common practice for them to dye their hair, use bronzers, and even, for those who can afford it, to have plastic surgery. The cosmetic industry has stepped up its campaign to attract male consumers to capitalize on their relatively new interest in cosmetic and treatment products. Believe us, they've been successful.

Having read all this about your outer package, now view it in perspective. The most important thing is how you do your job. Good grooming and manners are glamour niceties; doing the best job you can is a necessity.

Now for the inner you. Few of us are innately so self-confident that the process of job hunting doesn't trigger a fear of rejection. Psychologically, being evaluated in an interview touches a sensitive chord. Most job hunters feel particularly vulnerable, no matter how well qualified, at an interview, and there's a seemingly inescapable tendency to want to please the interviewer at any cost. Some of the world's most beautiful and successful models tell us that, as they wait to be interviewed for jobs and see the other beautiful models going in and out of the producer's office, they fall apart. "What am I doing here? I'll never get the job." And when they do, inevitably, *get* the job? "I'll never work again." It's a universal problem, not just yours and ours.

It's time, then, for the power of positive thinking. Remember, an interview is a two-way street. While they're interviewing you, you have an equal chance to evaluate them. Certainly they're in a position to reject you for the job, but you can reject the job as well. In terms of building self-confidence, there's nothing quite like knowing it's as much up to you as up to them. If you view the job-hunting process as a mutual one, involving a mutual assessment of advantages and disadvantages, you'll be way ahead of the game. It's the same principle that operates to make us incredibly successful with the men we're not sure we want, while we're completely tongue-tied around the men we have crushes on. When you're calm and serene, nerves under control, you project a self-assurance that will prove enormously effective to your total "package."

SELL YOURSELF

Here's where the action really begins. Self-analysis and introspection can only lead to a realistic career evaluation when you reconcile your perception of yourself with the way in which others perceive you. But what you must know is that *you* control this process. People form opinions about you from the input you provide. People react to how you behave, how you present yourself. What you say and what you show about yourself determines how people feel about you. No wicked fairy godmother can turn a sunny disposition sour. No *deus ex machina* controls your fate. You really are who and what you want to be. Werner Erhard of "est" has made a reputation training people to understand that simple fact. What is, is, and what happens to you, you make happen.

What we will do is try to show you how to present yourself in the most positive, saleable manner. And then give you our best advice to help you get *into* the situation where you have an opportunity to make your sale (get the job).

Your Resume

The first thing most prospective employers will know about you is what your resumé tells them. The purpose of a resumé is to provide someone with a short, informative profile on your experience, to see if you sound worth interviewing. It's a door opener, nothing more. A resumé won't get you a job. It's intended to make someone want to meet you, so don't fall into the trap of giving more information than is absolutely necessary. All an employer wants is pertinent background information about your experience and your abilities. So keep it short. That's rule one. And we do mean only one page. At this point, you probably don't have enough experience to make your resumé much longer than a page anyway. Many long-time careerists we've encountered still keep their resumés to one page, eliminating non-relevant-to-*that*-job material. There's plenty of time in an interview to fill in fascinating details.

Next, avoid "biographical" data. Your age and marital status are no one's business. Besides, you don't know what personal biases the readers of your resumé may have. They may think they want someone "mature" for a particular job, and not realize how level-headed a 20-year-old can be until they meet *you*. Or they may be convinced that a married woman can't expend the time and energy they'll demand, until you change their minds in an interview. The point is, you can't guess what they've envisioned in their minds, so don't get yourself ruled out beforehand. In addition, professionals often keep the resumés of promising candidates. There's a glamour industry grapevine. When the word goes out that someone is looking to fill a position, friends check their cache of resumés for each other. A resumé that doesn't stereotype you in someone's mind is good in this case, because you will not be thought of only in terms of the specific job you were interviewed for.

Be neat. Not fancy, just neat. There's no need to have your resumé engraved. Just see to it that it's as visually organized as you can make it. It should line up perfectly, and have no typos or misspelled words; there's no excuse for that! Careless errors can turn off a future employer faster than anything else we know. If it looks as if you didn't care enough to take the time to make your resumé crisp and neat, people are justified in thinking your work won't be crisp and neat. Hallmark has the right idea: "Care enough to send the very best."

The tone of your resumé should be positive. You want to show what you've been able to accomplish and indicate how your abilities can be useful to a given company. The most common format is a chronological resumé. Your name and address are placed on the top of the page. Then, beginning with your most recent job, list the dates of employment on the left, and the company name, job title, and a short job description on the right. List all your past jobs in descending order. Your academic background comes last.

Mention your degree and your major if that's pertinent, and any special abilities, like other languages. Forget all the extracurricular activities and prizes unless you're a recent graduate. As we said before, you can add a lot of things—including what you did in college—during the interview. A resumé just isn't the place for it.

If you've never worked, or have very little in the way of listable job experience, you might find it advantageous to use a "functional" resumé. With this format, you list your skill on the left and how you've used it on the right. This kind of resumé is often easier to work with if you've done a lot of varied, non-paying things, such as community work, political campaigns, charity drives. Incidentally, when referring to volunteer work, you should use the phrase "donated services," rather than "volunteer." It communicates the fact that you consider your time to be valuable. If *you* don't, who will? It's a small point, but serves an important purpose.

Never start a resumé with a discussion of your objective. That's less relevant to the employer than his own objective. Never include a picture. There's absolutely no need to say "references furnished on request." However, you might think about whom you'd like to use as a reference, should one be necessary. Then if you're asked, you'll have a ready answer. Here, it's best to use previous employers or people you've worked with (when you donated your services) or professors (if you're just out of school) in a related field.

INFORM YOURSELF

Even though you're a beginner and can't be expected to know the inner workings of the glamour field you're interested in, there's no percentage in being less informed than necessary. No one can give you experience you haven't had, but you can learn certain things in advance. Starting now, you should read some of the business and trade papers relevant to your career. And read them regularly. At first, it may read like a foreign language with names, jargon and information you've never heard before. Stick with it until you make it a habit. You really have no idea how much it will help you. You will sound knowledgeable to prospective employers, for one thing. Basic reading should include the business page of the largest daily in your city, the business column of at least one of the weekly national magazines, and at least one trade paper—the more the better. Since subscriptions can be costly (*Women's Wear Daily*, for example, now costs $48 per year), you should develop a working acquaintanceship with your local library. It might be smart to split a subscription with friends or roommates and to share the cost and the information. One of you, for example, could subscribe to *Women's Wear*, the other to *Advertising Age*. Mark in red what's of interest to your co-subscriber in *your* paper and have her do the same in hers. If you're going to the library, bring a friend. It'll be much more fun for you, and you'll get twice as much accomplished.

Of course, there are also special courses you can take and professional groups you can join. If you're ambitious, you should use every opportunity to meet people and broaden your horizons, provided you don't exhaust yourself. We all mean to accomplish more with our free time than we do, and we know that the road to hell is paved with good intentions (as our piano teacher endlessly chided us when we said we meant to practice). But reading the trade papers falls into a different category. If you want a career, it's essential.

1957929

THREE

❧ Down to Brass Tacks

Now that you've primed your inner self and outer package, now that you have a pretty good idea of what you think are your saleable assets, now that you're armed for job interviews . . . now what? Start looking, that's what. The most obvious and often the best place to look is in the want ads of the major newspaper in your city, or in the city where you've chosen to work. Don't sniff your nose at the want ads. A terrific theatrical agent we met recently told us, "I got my first job through the *New York Times*." She giggled. "Sounds like an ad, doesn't it?"

Emily is one of those slim, fair-haired, scrubbed, natural wonders born with what has become known as the "American girl" look. She told us she started looking for a job with no skills and no college, only the need to work and a desire to be connected with show business. She had wanted to be an actress, but realized, early on, that she couldn't take the insecurity and rejection involved. So, she leafed through the want ads in the New York papers, and found an ad for a "Gal Friday to a theatrical agent." When she applied for the job, she was asked if she could take shorthand. "No, but I can write fast longhand." Could she type at all? "Yes!" "You're hired." Just like that. It may not happen all the time, but we wanted to lay to rest the canard that you can only find pedestrian jobs in the want ads.

Newspapers are full of possibilities if you're diligent. You may find that the best *sounding* ads will be for jobs placed through personnel agencies. For a job hunter, there's no way around them. Since many companies depend on personnel agencies, you'll have to, too.

We suggest that you skim through *all* the jobs once or twice, so that you learn where to look. The age-old custom of separating male from female is almost entirely extinct. If the paper you're reading does separate them, move to a larger city; the one you're in is clinging to the past. (Well, if you can't move, then pay no attention to the separation. Answer any ad that appeals to you, even if it stipulates "male.") For beginners, the best selections are usually listed under administrative assistant, college grad, gal/man Friday (in deference to our new age of equality), or that old stand-by, secretary. Also, look under each glamour industry: advertising, public relations, broadcasting, radio, TV, publishing, editor (what you're looking for here is "editorial assistant"), marketing, and so on. Always read the want ads thoroughly on Sunday; it's the best day to look. Pretty soon you'll have a good picture of where good starting jobs are listed and what they're paying in the fields that interest you.

If you have non-glamour work experience, or have worked in a past incarnation, you should pay attention to some of the more advanced sounding jobs. You may not qualify, but you'll never know unless you try.

Read the ads with your trusty pen in hand, and circle anything that sounds even remotely possible. There are those who'll tell you to avoid ads saying things like "dreamy boss" or "plush surroundings" as being places where that's what the job has to offer rather than "room for advancement" or "great experience." But don't skip anything until you've tried it yourself. Some personnel agencies, despite their lush-sounding advertisements for not-so-lush positions, may have entrée to companies with good jobs, too. So, let them send you to the interview. Once you're there, you can tell the company's personnel person that you're only interested in a job with a future. The one category we'd advise you to omit completely is "receptionist." We suppose it's been done, but it is terribly hard to impress anyone as possessing "star potential" if all you do is sit at a desk and announce visitors.

Now you've circled a number of ads, some with box numbers, others with phone numbers. Obviously, you send your resumé—with a covering note—to the box numbers, and call the phone numbers. You're responding to an ad in Sunday's paper for a "chief cook and bottle washer." Write that you're very interested in pursuing a career in bottle washing and your resumé is attached (or you'd like to come in and meet with someone there). Don't try to dazzle. Just get an appointment. The more ads you answer, the sooner you'll learn the ropes. It's like learning to ride a bicycle; you've got to do it yourself. You'll find out pretty quickly which agencies treat you like a person and which see you strictly in terms of your typing speed and shorthand. You'll also find out which companies, hawking phony land deals in Arizona, run those tantalizing ads each week under "college grad., great career potential for self-starter." You'll have some horrid interviews. A job description may prove misleading or an interviewer may treat you in a demeaning manner. If you *are* treated badly, remind yourself that the interviewer has a problem, not you.

Our advice is not to be overly discriminating at the beginning. You need practice because, inevitably, you're going to make a lot of mistakes. So, go to as many interviews as you can. You'll get better as you interview more. You're in training and sometimes you'll feel as if you've been put through a wringer, but do it, and don't let yourself be discouraged. In each interview, you'll learn something new. You can try out different responses to the different kinds of questions you'll be asked. You'll practice your typing under stress and on lots of different machines. And you'll learn how to smile when your feet are killing you. So, wear comfortable shoes and pound the pavement.

You needn't let on that you're going to interviews for every job in town. Particularly with personnel agencies. You should walk a fine line between being an eager job hunter and being so "hungry" that the agency can bend you into a pretzel. Remember, it's the personnel agency's job to place people. That's how they make their money. They're not likely to tell you to hold out for a better offer. Their game is to convince you that you're not really qualified to do much of anything, that without them you'd probably never find a job. As a rule, personnel agencies are not exactly confidence builders; they tend to play on one's insecurities. That way, when you do get an offer—any offer—you're too relieved not to accept it.

The personnel business is making a genuine effort to upgrade and regulate itself. There probably are lots of super personnel people, some of whom may become your friends and allies over the years. The simple truth, though, is that the best people at personnel agencies deal with upper-level jobs (bigger salaries which command larger commissions) and you undoubtedly won't meet them your first time out. The agents you'll meet are either just starting out themselves or have not developed the savvy to deal with upper-echelon positions. With luck, you'll encounter some of the nice, helpful headhunters (as they're affectionately called) in the business. We just wanted your flagging egos to be prepared in case you meet the "downers." If and when you do find someone terrific in personnel, keep in touch, even if you find your job through someone else. Someone good will probably move up in the headhunting business, as you move up in your field. If you keep the contact, you can move up together.

The elite in the personnel field are the "executive recruiters." They are hired by companies to find top talent and usually work on retainer, not commission.

You won't get to meet them until they come looking for you. Still, if you're switching fields and know—or have entrée to—a good recruiter, call and ask for "advice" about making the switch. Recruiters have good business connections, and may well be able to give you introductions directly into companies that interest you, even if the jobs they are handling are out of your league.

WHO DO YOU KNOW?

Answering the want ads is a necessary Step 1 for getting the feel of the job market and for getting some experience under your belt. Personal contacts are Step 2. Available jobs are advertised, but hundreds and thousands of jobs are filled through word-of-mouth. Some of the best positions never appear in the want ads and never find their way to the desks of personnel agencies. Companies, not surprisingly, are happy to save the fee and find someone quickly at the same time. If you have friends, or friends of friends, who are working in fields you'd like to get into, call them. They'll know who you should see in their company or may know of an opening where you can meet your prospective boss directly. Executives seldom ask other executives about finding an assistant; they're more likely to ask other assistants in the company if they "know anybody."

Try to think of everyone you know. Talk to anyone who will talk to you. If your Uncle Irv knows a man in advertising who's willing to talk to you because he likes to help young people starting out (or just because he likes Uncle Irv), call him. Don't be shy. The worst thing he can say to you is that he doesn't have the time to see you. If that's the case, thank him and send him your resumé with a personal note. You'll be astonished at how many really nice people there are who will find time to see beginners, and who will go out of their way to be helpful. They probably started at the bottom and can remember how tough it was. We assume you'll remember, too, as you go up the ladder.

If you already have important contacts, don't try to "do it on your own." If Daddy knows the publisher of the largest newspaper in town, have him get you an interview with someone on the paper. And if Daddy owns the paper, please, don't launch your independence campaign right now. Use every bit of influence you can muster. And, if you're hesitant, bear in mind that influence can only get you the interview, not the job. *You* get yourself the job. A contact is a valuable door-opener, that's all.

Sometimes, people you know only slightly can help. Think hard about people who've crossed your path, one way or another. Maybe when you were a camp counselor several summers ago, one of the campers' parents was a buyer at a department store near you. Don't be afraid they won't remember you. Who cares? You can remind them. It's not unreasonable to call. Some people will turn you over to someone else (terrific! you've got a live body to talk to); some might be rude to you; but most people will be nicer and more helpful than you could have imagined.

Often, your contact will start off by saying, "Well, there's rarely anything open here." That's just to get them off the hook. Your reply should be: "Oh, I understand that. I just hoped you could spend a few minutes with me. I have a few questions about the business, and would appreciate any advice you can give me." If there's no advice forthcoming, don't hang up without asking if he/she can suggest anyone else you could call.

Don't give up if you can't find an acquaintance to help you. There are other avenues worth exploring. College placement offices are happy to help you. Many of them keep in touch with their alumni for this very purpose; all of them have their ears to the ground. Also, industry trade associations often know about companies with good training programs or internships. As a matter of fact, if you're still in school, you might contact these associations about a summer job. As you know by now, the summer jobs worth having are few and far between; but if the industry of your choice *does* have any special summer employment arrangements, its trade association will know. You've only got an outside chance, but why not try?

The important thing is not to be lazy about job hunting. It's really full-time employment, without pay. But there is a payoff—a job, first of all—and you'll have been "seasoned." You'll find that the process of looking for a job—going from office to office, talking to new people, articulating your goals—will erode some of that green, wet-behind-the-ears surface. You'll begin to look and act like part of the working world.

In the course of looking for a job, you're going to meet dozens of people. The fact that you won't work for them all doesn't mean you should forget them, or that you should allow them to forget you. A wise friend of ours is fond of saying, "There are only three hundred people in this world and, eventually, you get to know all of them." It's particularly true in the glamour industries. Everybody seems to know everybody or has heard of them. So, even now, when you're looking for your first job, you're liable to meet people who will become important to your career later. We're not suggesting that you transform yourself into some kind of calculating Machiavelli, but it would indeed be foolish to be unaware that knowing the right people in the right places can be enormously helpful to your career. If the vibes are good, if you like the people in question, it makes sense to keep in touch with them.

How? Let's say you've been interviewed by someone you liked, or thought was particularly bright or helpful. Write that person a thank-you note, expressing your appreciation for their time and suggestions. If you've found a job elsewhere, you might mention what you're doing. Be short and sweet. Everyone likes a thoughtful gesture, and it's a way of reestablishing your name in someone's memory.

As you go along in your working life, even more people will cross your path. Co-workers will move to other companies. You may move to other companies.

Obviously, you don't want to maintain contact with everyone. But with some, it's good business. Make no mistake about it, the people you know can be an important part of your success. Example: the accessories buyer at a large department store, who originally encouraged you but said more experience was required for the job, might wind up as accessories editor of a fashion magazine in three years. Who knows? By then maybe you'll be interested in working on that magazine. If you remembered to write her a congratulatory note when you read in the paper about her new assignment, she'll be more likely to remember you, and there's a good chance she'll be happy to see you about · a job. There's no guarantee she'll hire you. But she'll at least think of you kindly.

This is not a "using" people, buttering-up process. It's a legitimate business practice. One of the most successful salesmen we've ever known owed his success in no small way to his hundreds of friends (read "contacts"). A wedding, birth, illness, graduation never passed without some letter or phone call from Sam Salesman. We think that's overdoing it a bit, but the principle is clear. People respond positively to even the smallest tokens of thoughtfulness. The fact that it's not totally altruistic doesn't diminish the thought.

KEEPING YOUR HEAD ABOVE WATER

If you've followed our advice so far, and have called, written, and contacted every "possible," you're likely to find yourself drowning in a sea of names, addresses, and requests to "please call back." Example: "I'm sorry, Mrs. Smith is out of town till Tuesday. Can you call back then?" (By the way, don't call her Tuesday; she'll undoubtedly be swamped her first day back. Wait until Wednesday.) This is the time that the card file we mentioned comes in handy.

Every contact you make should be recorded, with the results, on its own card. If you send your resumé to Company X, put the date you sent it on that company's card, with a note to follow up with a phone call the next week. Remember to make a note to that effect on your calendar, or you'll forget. It's important to work with both a card file and your datebook. Otherwise, you'll find yourself pouring through an ever-expanding card file, trying to keep track of what to do next about which job. Your card file should not only list the names of the people you've spoken to directly at a given company or agency, but also the names of people mentioned in the interview. "Mr. Jones in casting may need an assistant, or Ms. Hill in production is looking for a gal Friday." Then, if the name comes up again, you won't think Hill is in casting. We all have a tendency to think we can remember more than we really can, that we'll be able to reconstruct events if we want to. Well, if you're job hunting properly, you'll be making too many contacts to keep them straight without a decent system.

There are two critical variables in the job hunting process. One is the size of the city you're looking for a job in. New York is obviously big enough to keep any job seeker busy with interviews for a long time. So are other big cities, but if you're looking for a job in a smaller place, don't get discouraged if things move slowly. The other thing is to be sure to pace yourself properly. If you're not temperamentally suited to rushing around from appointment to appointment, you'll begin to feel terribly pressured, and then you won't be at your best. It's very important for you to be realistic about how much can be accomplished in any one day.

Take it easy at first. Don't schedule your interviews too close to one another. You don't want to have your mind on your last interview and your eye on the clock for the next when you're talking to a prospective employer. They'll sense your tension. If you can, start with two appointments a day, one in the morning and one after lunch. You can probably handle the routine personnel agency interviews on a more crowded schedule, but don't overload yourself. Careers take time to build.

And while we're on the subject of scheduling appointments, now may be as good a time as any to discuss the psychology of when to make your phone calls. Each person you telephone has individual habits. Some people get to the office very early and like to take calls before ten, when things get busy. Others start later, and prefer to talk on the phone when things begin to wind down, after 4:30. Maybe you'll be lucky and reach people right off the bat. However, many women we've spoken to are amazed at how hard it is to get through to people. "They're always out. Sometimes I think all the people who've interviewed me know each other and that they're all in joint conference when I call." We know the feeling. But people who work have jobs to do. And they do go to an incredible number of meetings, conferences, or whatever their secretaries like to call them. They often can't take time, in the middle of a hectic day, to take the less important calls. (Face it, that's you.) So, when asked if you can call back, say "yes" and ask "what would be a convenient time?" It's conceivable that what *seemed* to be a convenient time for you to call back turns out not to be. Try again. Persistence pays off. Pestering doesn't. It's a fine line, but don't cross it. Maybe, after a few "please call another time" suggestions, you might drop the person a note. In general, don't expect *them* to call you. They're busy; they forget.

A perfect instance of this would be the story of Amy's summer job. She was hired for a specific project at one of the national television stations. She was more than eager to continue the job after the project was finished. They said, "We'll let you know." Days inched into weeks, and she waited. Finally, she called. "Oh," they said, "didn't someone call you? Let us check what's happening and we'll get back to you." Needless to say, they didn't, but Amy did. She waited three days and called again. Her persistence paid off. "Someone just dropped out," they said. "You start again tomorrow!"

When someone offers to see you as a favor (especially if there's no particular job in mind), be sure to make the appointment at *their* convenience. And offer to call to confirm it, in case something comes up for them. If something does come up, make a new date cheerfully and confirm again. Be philosophical about endless cancellations; they'll get to you eventually. They're doing you a favor and you should indicate that you understand how busy their schedule is and how much you appreciate the fact that they're willing to take the time to see you at all. Let them know you'll be delighted to see them whenever things slow down. Don't be pushy if they're obviously trying to avoid you. Otherwise, no matter how many cancellations, remember you need them!

THE ADVANTAGES OF TEMPORARY EMPLOYMENT

The best of all possible worlds would be to try out a job before taking it. Well, it can be done. There are agencies which specialize in temporary jobs, two days here (the secretary is out sick), a week there (we need help with inventory). It's like getting the chance to test-drive a company to see if the ride's to your liking, or trying on a particular office routine to see how it fits. Some of the best jobs around grow out of temporary employment. It's one of the smartest ways we know of to get your foot in the door. You will have entrée to almost any company that interests you since most organizations hire temps from time to time, and more often than not a temporary job mushrooms into something better and more permanent. That is, if you want it to. If not, you're free to go on to the next job.

Places that might ordinarily be closed to you without influence or contacts or without a graduate degree often have temporary jobs available. One of our brothers got a "temp" job with Ogilvy & Mather the summer he graduated from Swarthmore. The agency needed help with a special research project. He told us, "I noticed that there was plush carpeting on the floors and everyone looked very well-fed. I figured it was a good place to work. So, when my job was finished, I walked down the hall and poked my nose into every office, asking if anyone needed help with anything. One man said 'yes,' and I was in." What was so remarkable is that ordinarily Ogilvy & Mather doesn't hire anyone without an MBA for the kind of job he landed. See what we mean?

If ever there was a way to stand out in a crowd, to show what stuff you've got, a temp job is the answer. Most people who apply to temp agencies are either secretaries who aren't good enough to keep a job or people who don't want to commit all their energies to full-time work. To be perfectly candid, many temps are barely mediocre. Look at the position this puts you in. Willing to work hard, eager, enthusiastic. Employers will faint with glee when you show up. Well, almost. They're usually expecting the run-of-the-mill, "I'll do enough to get by" person. It's a golden opportunity to prove what you can do.

People hire temporary help for several reasons. Either someone is out of the office or on vacation, or the company is overloaded at that point, and needs additional help. The latter is the situation career dreams are made on. Either case gives you the break you're looking for—a chance to see and be seen. There's no better way for you to find out how you feel about one industry versus another, one company versus another. And it's an open sesame to jobs usually unavailable without personal contacts. One executive assistant at a national broadcasting station told us the best way in was to know someone. "Who'd you know?" we inquired. "Me? Oh, I got here through a temporary job." Q.E.D.

It's a good idea, then, to work at a variety of temp jobs until you get the feel of what you enjoy most. When you find an office that seems right for you, ask to stay. (If you're good, they're likely to ask you anyway.) If your immediate boss doesn't need you full-time, someone else in the organization might. If not right away, maybe something will turn up in a few weeks or months. Keep in touch. People are flattered that you want to work for them and will be impressed with your initiative if you're persistent but not a pest. If you prove yourself to be conscientious, cooperative, and efficient, you'll get an offer.

And the offers can be exciting. One friend of ours told us that every permanent job she's had started as a temp. And what jobs they were: she worked with Ben Hecht, the famous play-and-screen writer, spent two years in Rome with Dino De Laurentiis, the motion picture producer, had jobs at CBS, NBC, and so on. She literally chose her own spots. The jobs she wanted, she stayed with; the others she left when she'd worked the allotted time. There's no reason why you can't avail yourself of the same opportunity.

Last, but hardly least, taking temporary work is an ideal way to support yourself while you're trying other job-hunting techniques. It fits in neatly. You can still answer every ad that interests you. You can still follow every lead you get, and you're earning money at the same time. We're not sure why so few people think of this method for getting jobs, because it's one of the best. You won't feel the frustration of pounding the pavements day after day, either. You'll be gaining experience, making useful contacts, and earning a living to boot.

LEARN TO TYPE

Typing is an asset you should have, one more reason for someone to hire you. It's not true that if you can type well, you'll spend your whole life doing it. You may or may not need this skill in a beginning job, but it certainly can't hurt you. Whether you start your career as a secretary or not depends largely on what other talents or advanced degrees you've acquired. Throughout this book, we'll make references to different career paths; some develop out of secretarial jobs, others don't. The vast majority of women we've spoken to in the glamour industries, however, began as secretaries. They advised us that shorthand, or speedwriting, is often necessary in addition to typing. Every one of them verified the fact that good secretaries don't get stuck being secretaries. In exchange for doing their jobs well, they receive loyalty and support from their bosses, as well as a personal concern for their best interests.

Stacy is a good example. She's a warm, outgoing, down-to-earth young woman who is now associate producer of one of the longest running TV soap operas. We talked to her in the control booth during a break in rehearsal. Incidentally, every single person in that control room, from the producer on down, knew how to type. "You just never know when you'll be called on to pitch in," Stacy said. "I never went to college," she confessed. "My family had to struggle to send me to Katherine Gibbs Secretarial School after high school. They taught a lot more than typing and shorthand there. In a way, it was like a finishing school because we had to wear hats and gloves and dress just so. None of that jeans and T-shirt business. What they were after was to have us understand that appearance counts, too, not just how many words we could type a minute. Don't misunderstand me, there was plenty of emphasis on skills. As a matter of fact, after the demands made on us at Katie Gibbs, working was a cinch. To make a long story short, I landed a secretarial job at CBS. I was so thrilled to have a job in television that I practically begged for extra assignments. I thought they were doing me a favor just letting me work there. Another secretary, whom I'll call Barbara, started when I did. She had graduated from college with a major in communications and clearly resented her status as secretary. She thought she was too good for the job and was always putting me down for not having been to college and for being what she called an 'eager beaver'. Well, I ran into Barbara the other day. She told me she was a secretary at an ad agency now. I was delighted when she asked what I was doing. Barbara was dumbstruck. 'Who would have thought?' she blurted out. I just smiled a Cheshire cat grin."

The associate director of this same soap opera also started as a secretary at CBS with Stacy. She, too, had proved to be a hard-working dynamo, and they'd kept in touch over the years. It was perfectly natural for Stacy to contact her when the a.d. job became available. As we've said, keeping in touch with co-workers can prove beneficial in career terms. Both these women have terrific careers as a result of their excellent performance from the very beginning. Both agreed that the better you are as a secretary, the faster you'll be noticed and promoted.

You never know when you'll need secretarial skills even if your first job doesn't require them. Take a course if you have to. Everything you have to offer is just that much more for your employer to appreciate you for.

FOUR

⚼ *The Interview*

There's no way around it, the interview is *the* critical step in the job-hunting process. What goes before is in anticipation, what comes after is as a result. It may not make you comfortable to think of it this way, but the interview is when anything that is going to happen does or doesn't. Remember what we said in the "Sell Yourself" section: this is the time for mutual assessment. Consequently, each and every interview is important. Even the interviews that you know are for jobs you don't really want can be useful to you. Each interview is an opportunity to practice your ability to express yourself under pressure or reply aptly to unexpected questions. Each interview introduces you to one more person. Even if you and the job in question aren't right for each other, the interview can still prove helpful. Don't be cavalier in your attitude; prepare. Spend time thinking about the company and their business before you have the interview. Go to the library and see if any recent newspaper or magazine articles have mentioned the company in question, their close competitors, or their business in general.

Do your homework, even if it's a job that doesn't sound promising. You never know how you're going to feel about a job until you get the specifics. And, as we said, you never know whom your interviewer will know.

Remember two things. If you can get the interview, you can get the job. And everyone else out there is really no brighter than you are (probably less). You're up against unknown competition for every job, obviously; but don't assume the worst. It's possible that the applicant following you has more or better experience, but it's just as possible she'll have a laugh that drives the interviewer up the wall. If you know that you'll work harder, care more, and bring as much to the job as possible, you'll communicate that fact. That's what counts. Don't be overeager or overbearing. Just be confident. Even if you've never done the job before, be confident that you'll learn and do it well. They'll believe you if *you* believe you. If you doubt yourself, they'll doubt you, too. And believe us when we tell you that whatever it is, someone else has been doing it, which means that you can, too.

Probably the best advice we can give you about projecting a confident, serene image is to convince yourself that they'll be lucky if they hire you. After all, you know how much you want the job, how hard you'll work if you get it, how conscientious you are. Someone out there will count their blessings to put you on their payroll. Which brings up a very important question: Do you want the job?

A good interview, like most things in life between

two people, works both ways. A good job description is no insurance that the job will live up to it. Just because they can believe you doesn't mean you can always believe them. Not without asking questions, anyway. If the information you need is not forthcoming, ask lots of questions, but do it nicely. You're interested, but not pushy; curious, not nosy. Obviously, if you're interested in the job, you'll want to know many things. The *order* in which you ask your questions is important too.

HOW TO INTERVIEW YOUR INTERVIEWER

Begin with specific questions about the job itself. What exactly are the day-to-day responsibilities? Whom do you report to? Is your "boss" more than one person? How many? Whom does your boss report to? What does your boss's superior do? What you're trying to find out, of course, is whether the area you'll be working in, learning the ropes of, is right for you. Don't seem too inquisitive about jobs better than the one you're trying to get. That might give the impression that you're more interested in moving up than in doing the best job possible in the position under discussion. What you're after is the general "lay of the land."

It makes good sense to ask, also, about the company itself. Is it a pleasant, relaxed place to work? Is it hectic, frenetic, pressured? This is critical information to have; you're going to spend a lot of time there, and if the pace is out of kilter with your personality, disaster looms ahead. It's important to be honest with yourself and the interviewer. Some people thrive on chaos; others shrivel up inside unless things run with reasonable order and efficiency. A mismatch serves nobody's purpose.

Next, you might ask about the company's business. It pays to do some advance homework, so that you'll know a little about what that company does. Is it a new firm, just starting? Have they been absorbed into a conglomerate? Is theirs the new product you've been reading about in the papers? You know the kind of informed, intelligent questions we mean. If you're thinking of working for them, you should try to find out *something* about what they do and why.

At this point in the interview, you should be able to get some reading as to how you feel about the job. Does it really interest you? You should also be able to sense if your interviewer has positive feelings about you. If so, now would be the strategic time to ask about chances for promotion and getting ahead. Go lightly, because you don't want to seem heavy-handed. But you are entitled to know. If you're going to be interviewed by more than one person in a given company, you'll have to judge which interviewer is most likely to know the answers to certain questions. For example, a magazine's personnel department may know company policy on vacations and pay raises, but the editor you're going to work for will be in a better position to discuss when you'll get the chance to write or help cover the market. It is perfectly appropriate to ask these questions, once you've made it clear that you understand you're being interviewed for an assistant's job and intend to be the most fabulous one they've ever had.

The area of promotion and raises is probably the most delicate for beginners. But companies, big and little, know that to attract the best people they must offer opportunities for advancement. So, naturally, if you're bright and ambitious, you'll want to move up. Be aware that if what your prospective boss wants is a crackerjack secretary, he or she doesn't want to take the time to train you, show you the ropes, and get you settled in, only to have you chafing at the bit the minute you know how to do the job. Make it clear that you're eager to learn as much as possible, that you're happy to fetch and carry, go for coffee, stand at the Xerox machine, and so on. That you'll do what is required, and then some, but that you want to move up eventually.

The final group of questions to ask concerns company benefits: health care, vacation time and holiday pay, special training programs, company savings plans, tuition assistance, and so on. We don't suggest asking these specific things on a first interview (unless they're planning to hire someone on the spot); but find out the answers before you accept the job. If the interview isn't going well, or you decide you'd hate the job, there's no point in getting these basics. Don't take these benefits for granted. Some companies are still terribly archaic in this area. Other companies offer fantastic fringe benefits that might offset meager starting salaries. You won't know until you ask.

Now that we've stressed all the questions you should ask, let's stop a minute. People love to hear themselves talk. And interviewers are people. Don't be so eager to put yourself across that you overpower your interviewer. Or worse, prevent him/her from being able to reveal things that might be very important for you to know. If you let the interviewer talk, many of your questions will get answered without your asking.

HOW TO FIELD THE TOUGH QUESTIONS

By tough questions, we mean the discriminatory ones. And, without a doubt, you'll get your share of them. Those questions range anywhere from "How emotional are you?" to "Have you any plans for becoming pregnant?" These are questions that men are just not asked. An interviewer is apt to get as personal as you allow. So beware and be smart.

First and foremost, you should know that such questions are almost always *illegal!* Eileen Stein, a Washington lawyer highly regarded for her expertise in these matters, informs us that Title VII of the Federal Civil Rights Act of 1964 specifically prohibits discrimination in employment based on sex, as well as race, religion, and national origin. Most states have similar laws. "Companies may not base their hiring decisions on how large a family you are planning to

have, on your marital status, on whether or not you
have attractive legs (unless, of course, you're being
hired to model hosiery), or on any other factors or
standards that would not be imposed on male applicants," says Eileen. All questions in a discriminatory
vein should be handled in any manner which makes
you comfortable. There are those activists among you
who might feel impelled to point out to an offending
interviewer that the questions are out of line, and anyone subjected to outrageous conduct should be aware
of the proper avenues of complaint—namely, to report
the incident to your state's Human Rights Commission, the Department of Labor, the National Employment Association, or the EEOC. Still, most of us (for
good or for ill) are more interested in an expedient
solution. What to do, on the spot, without making
waves. And that's what we'll concentrate on.

Now, just to demonstrate how misleading appear-
ances can be: We called a buttoned-up, button-down,
Ivy League-type personnel man of our acquaintance,
expecting to get the "chauvinist" line that we wanted
to counterattack. Surprise! It was from him that we
got the most direct and pertinent advice on the subject. "The best rule of thumb," he told us, "is to answer as fully as possible all job-related questions, and
keep replies to other questions very brief." For example, if you're single and are asked about any immediate marriage plans, there is no need to fill in the
interviewer with the current status of your social life.
A simple answer that states that any change in your
personal life is unlikely to affect your business life

should be sufficient. A woman with children is almost invariably asked what plans she's made for her family's care; and often there is the implication that there'll be on-the-job stress due to her family's adjustment to her absence. Don't go into the subject even with a sympathetic woman interviewer. Just smile, confidently, and assure whomever that your family is well provided for. When the questions get personal, you should be composed, direct, and concise.

Humor is often a good way to handle the questions we could live without. We don't mean cute or evasive, but humor is rarely out of place. Our longtime friend Muriel told us a spur-of-the-moment reply that still makes her smile. Years ago, she was being interviewed for a copywriting job at Revlon—a company renowned for its less-than-benign demands on its employees. A personnel man asked her the classic: "But how will your husband feel about the long hours, the late nights, even holidays, we expect from our employees?" Her answer said it all: "He'll love every penny of them!"

There are other forms of discrimination, too, and sometimes these are more insidious and somewhat harder to handle. We're referring to the mythology surrounding women in business. One might expect, with the preponderance of data refuting the tired old clichés, that people would be embarrassed to keep harping on them. But they're not, and they do. What are we talking about? Well, it's subtle. For example, there are attributes common to both men and women, but in men these qualities are viewed as positive, while in women they're negative. For instance, aggressive men are "good," aggressive women "bad." Or the descriptive word changes with the sex, i.e., men are "decisive," women are "impulsive"; men "stand their ground," women are "stubborn."

An interviewer may say something like "we've had women here, but we find that they're not really interested in getting involved with some of the more demanding assignments. Understandably, they would rather be sure they can be home on time." Your answer might be: "Well, *I'm* very interested in taking on all kinds of demanding tasks and I would be willing to work odd, or long, hours."

One other piece of advice here. Make note of *who* is asking these questions. If it's someone in personnel you'll never see again, answer and be done with it. If it's someone you'll be working with more closely, be wary. Note how persistent the questioning is. If it's obvious in the interview that this is a person with set ideas on "a woman's proper place" in the business world, you don't want the job. It can be like trying to reform an alcoholic. He won't change. Forget it. You don't need him. Leave him to his male colleagues, and let *them* cope.

KEEP YOUR EYES OPEN

It's hard to prove in an interview how alert and efficient you'll be on the job, but if the opportunity presents itself, grab it. Our friend Karen, a bright go-getter to say the least, had the good sense to make the most of an interview situation someone less perceptive might have missed.

"I heard that ABC was looking for a production assistant on the Phyllis Diller show," Karen told us. "The director agreed to see me first thing Monday morning. I was very nervous because it was my first interview for a job I really wanted. When I got to the studio, the director was barking out instructions in his rather severe Scandinavian accent. I waited for him to get to me and just tried to stay out of the way. During the ten minutes or so that I was waiting, I heard him ask for coffee several times. Then he asked what had happened to the coffee. When it still didn't appear, he complained quite loudly that he couldn't understand what was so complicated about getting one lousy cup of coffee. It was obvious he wasn't going to attend to me right then, so off I went in search of a coffee machine. I figured the ABC production studio must have one and I found it without much trouble. I got about five different cups (black, light, and varying shades in between) and brought them to him.

" 'What do you do here?' he asked, as I offered him his choice.

" 'Nothing yet. I'm here to see you about the P.A.'s job on the show.'

" 'Everybody out,' he yelled, and in seconds the control room was cleared, and I had my interview. He hired me on the spot. I often think that if someone on that set had been more on the ball, I'd never be a producer today."

The moral of the story is to keep your eyes open.

People want to hire someone who can anticipate their needs, someone who doesn't have to be told to do the obvious. Karen was lucky, of course, to get the chance to demonstrate these qualities at her interview. Keep it in mind. If you're observant, you might get the same opportunity.

INTERVIEWERS' PET PEEVES

One question we tried to ask of everyone we spoke to was: "What are your pet peeves?" The number-one response was: "People who aren't willing to start at the bottom." Everyone we spoke to, without exception, told us they steer clear of anyone who seems to be afraid to "get her hands dirty." To quote a busy editor, "I'm not being a princess when I want someone to bring me coffee. I have tremendous demands on my time and I need an assistant who'll help me when and where I need help. If that means coffee, I don't want to have to apologize." Good beginning jobs in the glamour industries are hard to come by. If you're not willing to start at the bottom, someone else will be. She'll get the job, not you.

Another factor here is that everyone we know, superstars included, started at the bottom. Their attitude, understandably, is why shouldn't you? And, why shouldn't you? Because you have a degree? So does your competition. Because you know you're more capable than the demands of the job seem to require? They know that too. A first job will teach you more than you can believe, no matter how menial it sounds. If you recognize these feelings in yourself, work on it. The wrong attitude won't help you land the job of your dreams, or launch the career you have in mind.

Pet peeve number two is people who come unprepared for their interview. We're not only talking about the kind of homework we suggested you do in the first part of this chapter. We've heard tales of women going into interviews without resumés, with no idea of what business the company is in, or what the qualifications are for the job. We understand that a personnel person can get the requirements wrong, and cause you embarrassment. Short of that, however, make certain you know as much as possible. If you don't, explain early in the interview that you know less than you'd like to about the company or job. Never go to an interview without a resumé, even if you had sent one in the mail. It's inconvenient for someone to have to search for it if they don't have it handy. Personnel may not have forwarded it, or they may have lost it. It's easier for the interviewer to ask you questions if your resumé is in front of her.

Grievance number three is people who show up for the interview looking unprofessional. That can mean sloppily dressed, casually dressed, lugging shopping bags, and so on. A senior editor at the *New York Times,* who did not seem to be someone who is hung up on these matters, told us she found it insulting. "That's not treating me the way I want to be treated." She is 100 percent right. You will be meeting many busy professionals whose time is very valuable. Your appearance and demeanor will let them know you understand that.

Finally, several people mentioned something that's more subtle. "Tell women to have a little modesty," a seasoned executive advised. "Other people have accomplished things before they hit the scene. It wouldn't hurt to acknowledge it." This came from a lady whose ego is not fragile, so we perked up our ears. Others echoed the sentiment in different ways. What it boils down to, we think, is that you have to temper your self-assurance with the knowledge that you do have a lot to learn. If you recognize that, people will be much more likely to want to teach you. The glamour world is not holding its breath, waiting for your arrival. However, you'll probably find there are more opportunities than you think, if you are realistic about what constitutes a good opportunity. If your attitude is one of optimism, self-confidence, eagerness, and a healthy dash of humility, you'll do just fine.

Job hunting is a slow process, so try not to be impatient. Often, you'll have several interviews with the same company, weeks apart. The first shot may just be a screening procedure to discover if you have the general qualifications required. If that's the case, don't be distressed if there's relatively little interaction between you and the interviewer. You'll get your chance to be charming next time around. If there *is* a waiting period between interviews, you might find it beneficial to find out as much as you can about the company. That way you'll sound pretty well informed to your second interviewer.

In the meantime, while you're waiting for that second go-round, you'll have the chance to continue your job hunting in other places. You never know what's around the corner. A delay in one job may open the door to an unexpected opportunity somewhere else. Just remember, *the biggest mistake you can make is to decide that you want the job before you know for sure that it's a job worth wanting!*

FIVE

✍ *If It's Right, You'll Know It*

If you're not turned on by the prospect of doing a job (every day, forty hours a week, one hundred sixty hours a month, etc.) in that place, with those people, it's not the job for you. One of the biggest traps in the job-hunting game is that everyone is so eager to get a job that they often lose sight of the most critical question: Is it a job worth wanting? There are several ways to determine whether the job you're after is, in fact, worth taking. You have to be able to evaluate the factors involved. Is it a dead end, even though the money sounds good? Is it really the chance of a lifetime? Is the boss someone you want to work for? We're going to give you some guidelines by which to make these judgments. Nevertheless, your decision will probably be based partly on some elements we haven't covered. So, up front, we're going to tell you to trust your instincts.

The Concise Oxford Dictionary defines *instinct* as "intuition, unconscious skill." It's that inner sense that notifies our intellect that something feels good or bad or whatever. All of us receive these messages. Too few of us rely on them enough. (We're somehow so busy rationalizing, we disregard our innate ability to size up the situation.) At any rate, when you walk into an office, you'll know if you're getting good vibes or not. You're going to have to get up early each morning to get there—does it strike you as a pleasant place to be? Does the work sound like fun? All the logic in the world can't help you if your *feelings* about the job are negative.

Obviously, the ideal job isn't always just waiting to be served to you on a silver platter. You may have to settle for less than Utopia. Or, perhaps, in order to get where you want to in your career, you'll have to take a first job that isn't quite right. Okay. Even then, it's important to feel happy about the atmosphere in the office, or to like the boss, or to be satisfied with the location. Something. Otherwise, it's wrong for you.

Gretchen is a crackerjack producer at an advertising agency. She was happily working at a top-notch ad agency when a friend of hers, who was Creative Director at another agency, offered her an irresistible opportunity. "He wanted me to head up his agency's TV production department," Gretchen told us. "You can imagine how flattered I was. It was a new, hot agency, and I'd have the chance to run a whole department. The money was fabulous. We met several times, at dinner, to finalize the details, and I had really made up my mind to take the job. How could I turn it down? All that was left to do was to meet the president of the agency. The appointment was set for Monday morning, and I walked on air all weekend.

But the minute I got to the office, I knew I could never work there. The offices were located in a terribly run-down building in a very bad neighborhood. I knew I'd dread going there every day." So Gretchen turned down the offer, title, money, and all. Foolhardy? We don't think so. We're not suggesting that plush surroundings or elegant locations are important to everyone; we just think they're something to consider. These things are important to some people; if you're one of them, be aware of it. If, like Gretchen, you would dread going to work every day, don't take the job. Beginners can't be choosers, true enough; but even beginners can weigh the good points against the bad points. Often the deciding factor will be instinct. Use it.

HOW TO EVALUATE
A JOB'S POTENTIAL

To be totally realistic, your first job is a stepping-stone. Whether you've never worked at all before, are switching fields, or are reentering the job market after years of not working, it's still a get-your-foot-in-the-door job. As such, it cannot be evaluated on the basis of things that might appear important later on (compensation, benefits, and the like). The job should be judged by these criteria:

1. How much can you learn?
2. How many areas of the company/industry will you be exposed to?

3. How good a spot is the job in terms of promotion?
4. How smart/willing-to-train-you is your boss?

Let's say you're interested in a career in fashion and have had two offers. One is as secretary to the fashion editor and her assistant on a top magazine. The pay is unspeakably bad, and you have observed that the current secretary does little more than fetch and carry. The big plus, however, is that the secretary has been promoted, after only ten months on the job, to assistant accessories editor. The other offer is as "fabric editor" for a pattern company. The salary is much better and the job itself sounds more interesting than just being a go-fer. The responsibilities would include "covering" the fabric market (collecting swatches from various fiber/fabric houses to be used in fashion forecasts by the senior editors.) Again, the big plus is that the senior editors started in what would be your job. Okay, which job do you take, and why?

On the surface, the second job looks better . . . except. Unless you already know that fabrics are fascinating to you, that the formative fashion stage is what interests you, we think you'd be better off accepting the first job. You'll be making less money, but you will be getting greater exposure to more areas of the fashion world. Both jobs are good; both offer ample opportunity for advancement. But the magazine job will enable you to learn about the fabric market (every fashion magazine has a fabric department), beauty,

Seventh Avenue (where the clothes are designed and manufactured), accessories, lingerie, and publishing. The second job is much more limiting. To reiterate, if fabrics are your main interest, terrific! Go ahead. Otherwise, take the job with broader horizons.

Another determining factor in taking a job is the boss. Some people will let you know right off the bat that what they want is a secretary and they have no time to train anybody. Others might stress what a great learning position you'll be in. What you want to do is to learn. *Never* go to work for someone who responds unfavorably to your questions about advancement.

Keep your eye open for a dynamic boss. He/she may not be the fanciest conversationalist you've ever met, but don't be fooled. It's the track record that counts. If you get a chance to work for a real dynamo, grab it. People who work for movers generally move with them. (Unless, remember, they fail our "willing-to-promote" test.) Another winner to watch for is the old pro. Life may not be as much fun as when you're working for a "young Turk," but will you ever learn! We can only liken it to our school days, when some of the best professors were the older, near-retirement people. They knew more, understood more, and gave us more of themselves than some of the younger, more exciting teachers. Working for a true professional is a treat and a privilege.

If you catch wind of a *genuine* assistant's job, that's a prize. You'll be lucky to land it. The real McCoy involves working very closely with your boss, almost as an alter ego. This boss will say, "You'll go every-where with me, do everything I do, and I'll give you as much responsibility and work as you can handle." If you like the person, you'll love being his/her assistant.

There are things to avoid, if possible, too. Never take a job where there has been no proof of promotion from that spot before you, unless it's a newly created position. Never take a job with people who don't believe in promoting from *within* the company.

Having painted the bed-of-roses situations to latch onto when you can, we'll now tell you what to do if you can't. You might take a job that strikes you as being somewhat limited (maybe even a bit dull), *if* it puts you in a promotable position. Or you might consider working for someone you don't like a lot, if that someone is able to teach you something and has *demonstrated* a talent for getting secretaries or assistants promoted. Or, third, you can work in an area related to your main field of interest, if you think such experience will prove useful. The important thing is not to lose sight of your goal, otherwise you'll be side-tracked and wasting time.

At the risk of endlessly repeating ourselves, the way up and out of any first job, be it a plum or not, is to be terrific at it. There's just no substitute for hard work. If you can make yourself indispensible, that's even better. Ah, you say, if I'm indispensible, they'll never promote me. Wrong. If you're that good, and have really proved yourself, they'll promote you to keep you.

HOW TO LEAVE YOUR JOB

If the job is right, you'll know it. True, but it may not be right forever. You can outgrow your job, get a better offer, any number of circumstances can make you decide it's time to move on. How you handle yourself in leaving is as important to your professional reputation as any other aspect of your business behavior. You *are* your reputation in the eyes of co-workers. You make a name for yourself early in your tenure at any office and either embellish or detract from it when you go. The ability to land your next position is directly proportionate to the quality of your references, which hinge on your reputation. The deciding factor in being chosen over someone else for a job can be what a previous boss says about you. The scales can tip in your favor if a prospective employer calls an ex-boss about you and hears: "I just wish I could find another like her. If you get her, you're lucky." If you've done your job well, you'll get that kind of reference. Leaving your job well will help insure it. What we mean is that your leave-taking should be done graciously, and that you should leave everything in your purview in order.

No matter what the reason for changing jobs, all of us daydream about what we're going to say when the time comes. It's one of the games people play to help them over the rough times. We plan different departure speeches, depending on our mood. Nevertheless, there's nothing to be gained by giving the boss a piece of your mind. It's smarter to make constructive suggestions while you're still on the job and can benefit from the results than to hurl some final invectives when you give notice. If there's no chance of changing things while you're there, it's pointless to carry on about it when you go. Don't delude yourself into thinking you're just trying to make life better for your successor; she, undoubtedly, can take care of herself. Any momentary satisfaction you might feel will be offset by the bad feelings you'll leave behind you.

If you've felt undervalued and under-utilized, and your new offer demonstrates that you're worth more in the marketplace, don't gloat. You needn't point out the error of their ways; stating the offer says it better than you can. A sense of "just desserts" is understandable, but nonproductive. Only you have something to lose if you make enemies when you quit your job. Let your soon to be ex-employers off the hook gracefully. Give your notice nicely; no one likes to be rejected, not even an organization. You'll be better off in the long run if you make this final phase of your job pleasant for everyone. It's a good time to strengthen positive feelings toward you, or alter negative ones. Find the kindest way to tell them you're leaving. There are only two basic methods for giving notice; one leaves the door open for a counter offer and the other doesn't.

Situation One: You've received a job offer for more money and greater responsibility and are tempted by it. You like your present company, however, and are very happy with them. What to do? Give your boss the chance to match the offer. All you have to do is mention the offer and say you'd be more than glad to stay if the company will meet, or come reasonably close, to what you've been offered. You must be prepared to leave, of course, if the company doesn't come through for you. You can't use a competitive offer as a bargaining lever unless you're prepared to take the consequences.

If you receive an offer you don't want to accept, but still would like your present company to know about it, turn down the offer and then tell your boss. You say you've just declined such-and-such, but it makes you realize you're in line for a raise or a promotion. Threatening to quit is no guarantee for bettering your current position. If you feel entitled to a raise, ask for it; if it's not forthcoming, start job hunting. Ultimatums such as "I'm going to resign if you don't do xyz" are likely to backfire. Nobody likes to be pushed to the wall, and more than likely they'll let you resign.

Situation Two: You've received an offer and intend to take it. State your resignation flatly. If you have no intention of being seduced into staying with your present company, it's just not fair to permit the boss to make a counter offer, only to have you turn it down. Such tactics may be good for your ego, but it's embarrassing to your boss.

In any case, it's wise to be as flexible as you can about when you plan to leave and what is to be accomplished before you go. When you accept an offer, tell the people that you want to give your current employers an extra week's notice if it's possible. Your new company will respect the fact that you're considerate. You can always take a vacation, or start the new job early, if your offer to stay the extra week isn't accepted.

You might volunteer to finish a project or two before you leave; it's above and beyond the call of duty, but your ex-boss will remember forever that you made a special effort. Leaving a detailed status report, staying late to help break in your replacement, and the like, adds to a lasting final impression.

Never use the fact that you're leaving as an excuse to break rules or abuse customs you would honor were you staying on the job. Don't take extra-long lunches or start coming in late and leaving early. Above all, don't air grievances; gossip runs through an office like a forest fire. This is the time for self-discipline. Coming through for the company, even to the bitter end, encourages them to come through for you. What's more, it's dignified, and professional—the kind of behavior which reflects well on you.

SIX

❧ *The Facts of Life*

The first thing to learn about a job is that employers pay employees to work, not for fun and games. And almost all first jobs have one thing in common: they're low on the totem pole. The work itself, at the beginning, could hardly be called glamorous. (Although a secretary we know told us she met Robert Redford, Dustin Hoffman, and Warren Beatty during the first week she worked at a major film studio.) Your given title may be secretary, but the job will often be go-fer . . . go-fer coffee, go-fer messages, go-fer almost anything you can think of. It's culture shock. In a matter of days, you go from editor of the school literary magazine to flunky; but you've got to pay your dues. Everybody does. You're really being paid while you learn the language, the business, what opportunities lie ahead (and what pitfalls). Starting at the bottom may not be glamorous, but neither is it the catastrophe that starting near the top can be—where the spotlight shines on you, your inexperience, and your mistakes. Viewed in that light, you'll adjust to your shift in status more easily.

LIFE AT THE BOTTOM

Needless to say, it's more amusing to contemplate life at the top, but that's not where your career begins. Let's talk about what life at the bottom really means. It doesn't matter whether you're just out of college or fresh out of motherhood, it's a jolt to find yourself back at the beginning of things, even though you acknowledge the fact that you're not equipped to start *above* the bottom rung. As a friend of ours aptly put it: "It's just that the bottom is so . . . lowly." There's little comfort for our egos to find that all we're expected to practice our competence on, all we're expected to utilize our education for, is the coffee machine, the typewriter, and becoming the best schlepper * in town. Resign yourself to it. Don't fight it; use it. That's right, use it. Leave all those pampered attitudes behind you. Learn to schlep with dignity and good humor and you'll have mastered the first important lesson in how to end up with a glamour job.

No matter what your past accomplishments are, you're back in the first grade. And if you're open to it, everyone you meet can be your teacher. You may not be making much money yet, but you're getting paid while you learn. Put a smile on your face and become the best secretary or assistant your boss ever had. That's the secret. The most willing at the bottom rise

* Schlep, from the German word *schleppen* (meaning "to drag"). A schlepper, loosely, is someone who drags or carries things from one place to another.

the most quickly to the top. Buyers begin selling behind the counter. (Saks Fifth Avenue's executive training program, incidentally, includes five weeks of selling.) Art directors start doing paste-ups. Designers first work as pattern fitters. Editorial assistants type other people's copy. Everyone's first job is more or less menial. If you work hard, you'll get your chance to demonstrate what you can do. But first you have to know your way around and fit smoothly into the routine of things. That's when you begin to be valuable. You'll find a lot of people ready to help you, too. But be wary. Competition is fierce in the business world. The woman at the next desk may be your friend and wish you well, but not more than she wishes herself well. A surprising number of people feel threatened by up and coming underlings with talent. Including your superiors. Deborah told us about two incidents in her early career:

"I started as a secretary, really, to one of the chief writers on a fashion magazine. Sara wasn't one of those fancy, hat-wearing magazine editors. She was young, lived in the Village, and I adored her. Well, Sara adopted me. She invited me to Thanksgiving dinner, introduced me to her eligible brother and became my mentor. She trained me, helped me, covered my mistakes for me, and gave me every opportunity in the book. Sara really is one of the most extraordinarily talented women I have ever known. Remember, everything she wrote (or rewrote for others on the staff) went through my typewriter. There seemed to be nothing she couldn't do—humor, editorials, interviews. I learned everything from her. Sara let me write blurbs and captions almost immediately. She would correct them and send them through under my name so I'd get credit. She's a unique lady and I'm beholden to her.

"Eventually, Sara was promoted to Senior Editor. Some time later, I was given the job she'd vacated. Needless to say, I was absolutely thrilled. I ran down the hall to share my triumph with Sara—after all, it was as much her doing as mine. I was so excited and grateful, and thought she'd be so pleased. I rushed into her office and blurted out the news. Her comment, ice cold: "Don't come to me for help." It took me years to understand what had happened. As her protegé, I guess, I could be lovable. The promotion had made me competition."

That's a pretty tough lesson to learn, but one worth noting. Don't expect Girl Scout values and idealistic standards from everyone you meet, or like, on the job. When you find them, it's a bonus. The other incident Deborah described is also not the only one of its kind to happen in the history of the world. "This took place after Sara had moved up to Senior Editor, but before I'd been given her job. A trade-paper editor, named Evelyn, was hired to fill Sara's slot. She was a pleasant enough person, trying desperately to get over a painful divorce. Evelyn worked very hard, but she just couldn't do the job. Writing for a trade paper was obviously too different from magazine copy for her. At any rate, the editors were forever sending her copy back for rewrite. Now, keep in mind that Evelyn was my boss. Part of her job was to edit *my* copy. Well, you guessed it. She took to deleting phrases from my work and using it in hers. I couldn't believe it! Nothing in my life had ever prepared me for that!" "What'd you do about it?" we asked. "Absolutely nothing," Deborah answered. "It was one of the few times in my life that I was smart enough to keep my mouth shut. I suppose if it had gone on long enough, I might have exploded. But I decided to wait to see what happened. They fired her, eventually. And that's when I got the job. Would you believe, *she* was bitter!"

While Deborah didn't deliberately set out to let someone else get credit for her work, there are situations when a good assistant or secretary does just that for her boss. It can go with the territory. We had lunch with Betty the other day. Betty came to New York from Atlanta five years ago. We thought she was naive at first; that soft Southern manner and gentle personality can be misleading. Not that Betty isn't as kind and eager to please as she seems; it's just that she's aware that her positive outlook on life can be a tremendous asset. Today, she's earning $35,000 a year as an account supervisor at an advertising agency, with two account execs and a secretary under her. That's a pretty rapid climb, and we asked her about it. Betty admitted that she'd been very lucky. "I started as secretary to two account execs at this agency. I loved it. I did everything I could think of to be helpful to them. And maybe they did take advantage of me. All the other secretaries told me that I was a fool, that I should try to take credit for some of the things I did instead of letting them pass off my work as their own. I don't mean to sound like Pollyanna, but I really wanted the experience." Betty told us she not only typed their reports, but asked to help research them as well. She dug up the background material they needed to write their marketing plans. She trudged to drugstores to do reports on competitive products. She took work home when she had to. "There's a policy here," Betty continued, "of recruiting assistant account executives from the MBA programs of the top schools. But when an assistant's spot opened up on my bosses' account, they really went to bat for me. They got the precedent suspended in my case, and I was on my way. You can make your own breaks a lot of the time."

Betty's hard work and good nature earned her the respect and support of her bosses. She was eager to do more than she had to; she wanted to learn and was happy for every opportunity that came her way. That's the key. You have to be able to recognize an opportunity when it appears and, then, you have to be ready to do something about it. A lucky break may speed up the process, but nobody gets to the top without earning it.

One other interesting point came up that day at lunch. Being a woman can be an advantage in business in some circumstances. To quote Betty again, "A man without an MBA has a very hard time getting into marketing. A woman can always start as somebody's secretary, and work her way up from there." The practice of hiring male secretaries is still very rare; silly, but true.

Our close friend Jeffrey (who first encouraged us to write this book and dreamed up the title) described the tough time he had breaking into advertising without a graduate degree. He is an uncommonly talented man of enormous wit. He's also very smart, and gutsy enough to approach a problem head on. He wanted a copywriting job at an ad agency. He made up a "book" of (imaginary) ads and took it to every agency willing to see him. "I finally got an interview at Wells, Rich." (That's Wells, Rich, Greene, the agency made famous by its brilliant founder, Mary Wells Lawrence, and known for its creative campaigns for Alka Seltzer —"I can't believe I ate the whole thing"—and Benson & Hedge's "silly millimeter longer.") "I was interviewed by a terrific creative director, who had just finished the Bic Banana campaign with Mel Brooks. She seemed to like my work, but told me the same thing I'd been hearing for weeks: 'We never hire juniors; get some experience and then come back to talk to me.' I was so frustrated. How can they expect you to get experience if no one will hire you? So I asked her how *she* got started. 'As a secretary,' she told me. 'So hire ME as a secretary,' I pleaded." Well, she didn't do that, but she did get Jeffrey a job in traffic. (That, by the way, doesn't explain why someone's late to work. The traffic department in an ad agency is responsible for scheduling creative work flow and insuring that production proceeds in time for deadlines.) Within a year, Jeffrey became a copywriter on the TWA account.

Now Jeffrey is a most unusual person. He knew he

had to try an unorthodox approach in order to get what he wanted. He had enough self-confidence to take a job that most male college graduates would consider "beneath" them. What's interesting is that even when men are willing to do whatever is required to get their feet in the door, it's hard to find an employer who will let them. We like to think that liberation works in all directions. Maybe men will be able to get some jobs that were traditionally women's. Why not?

One thing must be pretty clear, by now. Life at the bottom isn't a permanent state of affairs. If you work hard and are ready to withstand the slings and arrows, you'll move up. You'll know when you're ready and so will the boss. Just give it enough time.

THE NEW JOB BLUES

No one talks about it; articles on careers don't discuss it; it's not on the curriculum in business schools. But the new job blues are as widespread as colds in February. We've rarely encountered anyone who hasn't been afflicted at least once. Our dynamic friend Renée, who's a smashing success, phrased it this way: "Every new job is a whole new stomach-ache." Why is it so hush-hush? We're not really sure, but whatever the reason for secrecy, we want you to know about it and be prepared for it.

The symptoms sneak up on you, usually some time after you've settled in. You can expect to feel a smidgin anxious at the beginning, even though you're ecstatic about the new job. But just when things seem to be sailing along, when you're getting to know people's names and where things are, when you seem to be catching on to the routine . . . whammo! You begin to feel depressed, irritable, clumsy, left out. Your sense of humor fails you; your voice sounds too loud; your self-confidence fades. These are signs of the new job blues. The causes vary (and we'll discuss them) but we want you to know that the cure is patience and the knowledge that everyone else has been through it, too.

The three major culprits that can cause this misery are:

1. You need a friend.
2. You don't have enough to do.
3. You have too much to do, and not the vaguest notion how to do it.

The last is easiest to cure. The first takes a little longer, but you'll recuperate before you know it. The second is by far the most insidious and the hardest to handle. But let's take it from the top. You need a friend at work. It's lonely. Everyone else runs off to lunch and no one asks you to join in. Everyone gathers around the coffee machine, chattering about last night's activities or tomorrow evening's plans and nobody includes you in the conversation. You feel like an interloper, with two left feet. You tell yourself it's silly, but you feel rotten anyway. Just know that *everyone* feels like an outsider the first few weeks on the job. It always takes people time to get used to having a new face around (remember that, when you're a veteran and a new face enters your office). If you bide your time, the situation will straighten out. One clever gal we know made lunch dates with her college friends, her mother, her brother, and her Aunt Tillie for a month—just so she wouldn't be sitting there when everyone left at 12:30 P.M. She went about her business, being pleasant but not intrusive. It didn't take too long before someone popped in to ask her to lunch.

One word of caution; don't be overly eager to make your office friends into bosom buddies. It's taken you years to make your other friends. Go slowly about sharing confidences (if you want to be sure they'll be kept "confidences"). Be sure your newfound friend isn't a chronic gossip.

The second problem, not having enough to do, happens more frequently than you might imagine. Either you were hired for a new position that hasn't been worked into the organization yet (in which case, once again, bide your time), or you're working for someone who's been "kicked upstairs." More often than companies like to admit, an executive is "promoted" to a job of no real responsibility, either as a form of punishment (for refusing a transfer, say, or for not coming through on a major assignment), or as an expedient method of removing someone who can't be fired (to make room for a younger or better executive).

Maggie, a very eager assistant editor we know, related the following story to us. "I started as secretary to the 'special projects manager.' He seemed very nice and important, you know, big office and fancy desk, all the trappings. I probably should have asked him more about exactly what *he* did, but it never occurred to me. We mainly spoke about the company itself at the interview. And he asked me lots of questions about myself and my interests. He seemed more interested in *me* than in my typing speed, which impressed me. Anyhow, I took the job. For the first few weeks I was kept sort of busy straightening out the files, doing expense reports, typing a few letters. I thought he was breaking me in. But nothing happened. It began to take on the proportions of a nightmare. Here I was, on the executive floor, sitting outside Mr. X's office, one secretary in a line of six. All the other secretaries were pounding away at their typewriters, running around from department to department doing things. And I just sat there, with nothing to do. I'd come in, read the paper and then do the crossword puzzle. I was relieved when it came time to bring Mr. X his coffee. I was too embarrassed to ask the boss what *he* was doing all day, behind that closed door.

"Anyway, to make a long story short, I went to the head of personnel, who had hired me. She told me to be patient, that a better secretarial job would be coming along soon, and in the meantime it was all right to read a book in my free time. Mr. X, the personnel lady assured me, *did* work on special projects, but things were unusually slow just now. Let me tell you, I became the best-read person in town that year. Eventually, I was moved over to the senior editor's office." Was she sorry she'd stayed? "I'm not sorry now," Maggie assured us. "It was the worst year of my life. It's absolutely awful doing nothing day after day. But I got a great job as a result of it. The higher-ups felt they owed me something, and it's a super company and my new boss is a dynamo. Looking back, it didn't hurt me, but at the time it was terribly demoralizing."

It's highly unlikely, however, that you'll have to face such an extreme situation. If you have been hired for a newly created position, or work for someone who has been assigned to a new area, don't worry. The pace will pick up soon enough. For some inexplicable reason, it takes longer to fit in than anyone ever anticipates. You might be told to drop everything and start work immediately, only to find that you've got nothing to do at work for the first three weeks. It happens all the time, so try not to let it frustrate or anger you. It's not done deliberately. The company probably felt, honestly, that they couldn't survive without whatever services you'd been hired to provide. The wheels of efficiency turn with agonizing slowness. Just use the time to get your bearings. Possibly, you'll be able to spend some time working in related departments to see how they function. Be observant; just being around an organization can give you a chance to see how things are done. Before you know it, there'll be plenty of action.

The third cause of the new job blues is panic-button time. Here's the script. It's your second day on the job. You told them you didn't know anything about whatever it is they want you to do. Everyone is frantic and you're being counted on to come through in the crisis. But for the life of you, you aren't sure what they need, whom to ask for help, and what will happen if you foul it up. As the butterflies convene in your stomach and the tears well up in your eyes, all you can think of is that old phrase "baptism by fire." What to do? We know better than to suggest you relax. But take a deep breath and keep your head. You won't get fired; you're not really expected to be experienced. Just don't get in the way. Write down everything you're asked to do, because when instructions are shouted at you, in what seems at the time a foreign language, you'll forget. And you won't be stuck saying something inept-sounding like, "Well, he asked me to do something about the lights." You'll be able to ask a specific question. They understand you're just beginning; they just haven't time in a crisis to attend to you.

Our friend Ellen laughs, now, about her first week working for a photographer. She was hired as gal Friday to do odd jobs around the studio. This encompassed a variety of chores—calling in models on "go-sees," billing, ordering lunch on "shoot" days—nothing too complicated for a college graduate. Her first day at work, the photographer and his assistant were out on location, so she had time to familiarize herself with model agency names, his filing system, and the like. The next day, pandemonium! Twelve different shots had to be photographed *in* the studio. Usually, a crackerjack stylist assisted this talented but rather disorganized camera ace. Today, of course, the stylist was out sick. That she'd never missed a "shoot" before that day was little solace to Ellen. It was Ellen's responsibility to get the models ready and to make sure that everything necessary to the pictures was either on the girls, on the set, or somewhere in view. The photographer was frantic. His harried assistant was too busy to help Ellen, as he was involved with the technical details of each shot. The client was becoming hysterical. And even with her B.A. in English, Ellen couldn't decipher the stylist's notes.

"I spent the first hour just trying to match up the names and faces of the models. At that point, they all looked alike to me—gorgeous! I couldn't quite grasp the fact that it didn't matter how the models looked from the back, that the clothes could be pinned and so forth. So I wasted a precious half hour trying to switch models and outfits so they'd fit better. I didn't realize that a pair of too-big pants could be taken in with a clothes pin or a clip. And the models were so busy, they didn't notice. Everybody seemed to be screaming directions to me at the same time. It was a zoo! And I was sure I'd be fired there and then. The next day, I was lavished with praise for being such a good trooper and pitching right in, not even falling apart when I got yelled at! I learned more that day than any other single working day of my life."

We asked Ellen what she felt was the main thing for someone in a similar situation to remember. "You'll survive. That's the one thing to remember," advised Ellen. "You'll live through it. And no matter what mistakes you make, someone else has made worse ones. And when it's over, you'll feel closer to everyone, sort of like having been through the war together." It's true. Living through a crisis does bring people together. You become an insider long before you would have under more ordinary circumstances. So, keep calm.

In addition to those we've already mentioned, the new job blues can assume other guises, equally unexpected. Here again, we just want you to know about it, be prepared for it, not be surprised. There's the now-that-I've-got-the-job-can-I-do-it syndrome, for example. We're not sure what throwback to childhood brings about this onrush of self-doubt, but somehow as soon as someone lands a terrific job, it hits. And we're not just talking about beginners, we're talking about people well along into successful careers. From movie stars ("You're only as good as your last picture" is a well-known Hollywoodism) to account executives. "I'll never be able to do this!" is a familiar cry, no matter if it's something one is good at or smart enough to learn. All of a sudden, problems seem insurmountable and the person is riddled with a case of the jitters.

One eminently successful copywriter we spoke to (whose present position earns her in the neighborhood of $75,000 a year) told us that she went right into writer's block when promoted to her current job. "All I could think of," she said, "was that they'd find out I'm not worth that much money. I just sat there at my desk, unable to write a line. I drew a blank." She attributed the fact that she had a history of brilliant accomplishments to luck. Fortunately, her new company recognized the symptoms and sent her off on a week's paid vacation. When she returned to the office she was fine.

Most of us aren't quite that fortunate. We have to get our own heads straight, without assistance. The best thing to do is to accept the ailment for what it is, a case of nerves, and try to impose a little logic onto what is basically an emotional problem. Talk to yourself: you wouldn't have considered the job if it were way over your head; they wouldn't have hired you if you really weren't qualified. And, of course, you can handle it. Once again, your old friend Time will come to your rescue. Give yourself a chance; after a few weeks on the job, your insecurities undoubtedly will begin to fade. How can we be so definite? You're better than you think you are, for one thing. If you're bright, cooperative, and even moderately efficient, you'll find yourself a rarity.

There is a conspiracy of silence, almost a gentleman's agreement, about the incompetence in the business world. We think you should know about it now. You will be confronted (later, if not sooner) by waste, red tape, and a degree of inefficiency that heretofore you only associated with government bureaucracy. The resultant malaise, alas, you'll learn to accept. There's really very little to be done about it. You can try to change inefficient procedures, if they apply to you, but many companies are rooted in maintaining the status quo. That's how it's always been done and that's how it's gonna continue to be done. If we ran our private lives that way, it would be disastrous.

Horrible though it is to say, the truth of it is you'll

get used to it. You'll learn how to circumvent it when necessary, and how to cope with it the rest of the time. No matter where you work—some of the best, most famous companies have an equally famous level of incompetence—there will be a certain amount of inefficiency. The question is how much. Don't continue to work in a disaster area just because you now know industries get bogged down by red tape. Make suggestions for improvement, but don't be crestfallen if your ideas fall on pleasantly deaf ears.

There are lots of people who start out with high ideals and good intentions but lose them quickly when they see how easy it is to slide by with a lick and a promise. Exciting careers are not built on "sliding by." One woman we know is ready to swear her career was made "less on talent, because there were lots of people just as talented, and more on the fact that I could be relied on." If you really do your job properly, get all the details right so that your employers *know* they can depend on you, you'll go places. *You* don't have to get by just because your boss does. It's one way of becoming indispensable, incidentally. Despite the frustrations of dealing with idiotic filing systems and less-than-proficient co-workers or superiors, there is a silver lining to this particular cloud. You'll begin to recognize your own worth. Instead of wondering "Can I do that?" you'll be thinking, "If that dumdum can do it, so can I."

One final thought: don't be too unforgiving. All of us tend to cling a little rigidly to the *status quo ante*. It's comfortable, if cumbersome. Sometimes, it's more trouble (in time and money) to reorganize, or re-staff, than it's worth. An old friend of ours told us this story, on herself. "When I first worked for this company, I spent most of my time bitching about their triplicate filing system. It seemed so stupid and took so much time. The hours wasted, and the tons of needless papers nobody ever looked at, drove me bananas. When I was promoted, the girl who inherited my job spoke to me about our filing system. Would you believe I told her, 'That's how it's always been done. You'll get used to it.' I guess all of us are inclined to resist change."

The point of this whole chapter is to enlighten you, to tell you the truth, not to discourage you. Elsewhere in the book, you'll read about the fun, the glamour, the excitement, the things that make going to work each day a joy. But the facts of working life are not different from the facts of any other aspect of living; work is a mixture of terrific and not-so-super things. It's better to be prepared for what lies ahead than to be jolted into reality. Some wise person must have said somewhere that it's all right to have stars in your eyes as long as you've got your feet on the ground.

SEVEN

≥ *Career Building vs. Job Hopping*

There's a difference between career building and job hopping. The latter tends to be frivolous, often leads to disaster, and invariably is the result of indecisiveness. Career building is another cup of tea entirely. All roads don't have to lead to Rome directly. It isn't graven in stone that you must start at GO and move in a direct progression to a stated goal. In geometry, the shortest distance between two points is a straight line, but we all know that often the fastest route to a destination can be via detour. So, to begin with, it's helpful to know where you want to go in your career, then you can start laying the foundation. As you go along, you may find your ideas changing. Fine, change away. Just keep a weather eye on where you're heading, so you don't get sidetracked needlessly.

There's a fine line between loyalty and safety, and opportunism and challenge. You need to stay flexible and do what's best for you in the long run. Thus, from day one you've got to think *career*. From your very first job, you've got to keep in mind: how will this experience be useful? what doors does this job open?

will doing X help me get into a position to do Y? At this point you may have only a vague idea of where you think you'd like your career to lead. It's really still too early to nail down anything definite; you're entitled to change your mind anyway. But you must learn to think in long-range terms. Otherwise, you'll be unable to assess the possibilities as they come along.

The critical question to ask yourself: is the time you're going to put in well spent? The safe way may be to start as a secretary in a company, take your promotions as they come, and wait it out until you get to the top. Sometimes, however, it's quicker, more fun, and smarter to diversify a bit. Terrific careers are built in many different ways. Only you can decide, each step along the line, what's most propitious for *your* career.

There are pros and cons at every turn on the path to your career. There are successful adherents of the straight and narrow and big winners who subscribe to the winding detours route. It depends on who you are, which path appeals to you, what road is most comfortable for you, and the opportunities that come your way. Would you get bored staying in one place and waiting it out? Would it make you nervous, having to prove yourself all over again if you shifted jobs every three years or so? Circumstances will probably govern your decision as much as anything else. Circumstance and luck and timing (which is really a combination of the first two). We've divided the most common career paths into three categories: the straight line, the simple switch, and the building-block approach.

The Straight-Line Approach

This is the traditional success ladder. You start at the bottom and work your way to the top. True, it's less common in the glamour world, where playing switch sometimes seems like the most popular game in town. But staying power pays off, too. (In some companies, if you can hold on through the shifting tides of fortune at the upper echelons, you're almost guaranteed a top position eventually. No one admits this, of course, but it's true nonetheless.) There are certain advantages unique to this approach.

You learn the ropes, once. In other words, you catch on to the dos and don'ts of the organization, learn how to avoid getting caught in interoffice politics, understand the subtleties of the top-brass hierarchy, so you can just sail along smoothly. If a company's personality suits you, it pays to stay. For example: if you're an early riser and your company gives points for coming in early in the morning; or you like to take long lunches but don't mind working overtime, evenings, or weekends and top management does the same. Things like that add up to compatibility.

Your reputation builds. Once you've made a name for yourself, it sticks. (Remember what your mother said.) Reputations are made very early, so it's important to be on your best behavior from the outset. If you've always been responsible and reliable, when things foul up someone or something else will be blamed. If it *is* your fault, people will understand that anyone can slip up once in a while. On the other hand, if you have a reputation for not following through, the assumption will be that you're at fault—even if you were nowhere in sight. Once you've gained a good reputation, it stays with you. Once you're tagged as bad news, that will stay with you, too, and it's a very hard label to change. Waiting out promotions may not take as long as trying to prove yourself all over again in another organization.

You build equity. People too frequently overlook this obvious benefit in their hurry to attain success. Will that new job with the nice salary increase cost you two week's vacation? Will you lose out on profit sharing? Savings plans? Hospitalization coverage? Will you be fully "vested" in your present company soon and have to wait years where you're thinking of going? Just because you don't see the money in your paycheck every week doesn't mean that fringe benefits aren't real money. For many career-builders, the big money often comes from stock options and profit sharing. Make sure you know what you're doing when you sacrifice this hidden aspect of your salary for another job. It may still be too early for you to get in on this action. If your company does offer these kinds of benefits to long-term employees, however, it can mean more to you than a short-term salary increase.

Small disclaimer: A straight path doesn't have to

mean you literally never leave the company you started with. We consider people who start at the bottom of their profession and continue straight up, in the same line of work, as having pursued the straight-line approach. The General Merchandise Manager for a West Coast store has worked for three different stores over a period of twenty years. She began in the training program of one store, became a buyer, and stayed there five years. Then she moved to another store as senior buyer. She joined her present store eight years ago. Each move was a step up in money and prestige, well-timed to maximize the benefits to her career. She advises, "Sometimes you can only go so far where you are. It usually doesn't pay to be opportunistic, in the short run. But there are stages in any career where a move is invigorating and stimulating, mentally and financially. Sometimes you get typed in an organization if you stay too long. Sometimes, you can get stuck behind someone. Let's face it, changes keep us on our toes."

And there's the rub. The straight-line approach does have the dangerous pitfall of lulling us into complacency or laziness. You really shouldn't stay with a company because it's easier. Or because you're not *un*-happy. That, you'll regret later. Don't limit yourself because it's the line of least resistance. If you remain in a situation where you're comfortable, but not forced to grow, where it's easy but not stimulating, you'll get bored (and be boring). The really successful straight-line followers are those working in organizations that provide tremendous variety and challenge.

The Simple Switch

This path is really a first cousin to the straight-line route. It involves a logical shift to a closely related industry. People do it all the time without giving it much thought. Glamour industries are so closely inter-related that you can often move between them without a major career disruption. Being at one end of a business at one point in your career, then moving to another, can often broaden your background and thereby strengthen your credentials; and, not incidentally, turn you into a much more valuable commodity. A good example of the simple switch would be the move from an agency dealing with a company and that company. In advertising and public relations, this kind of lateral shift is *comme il faut.* Many executives look for people who've had experience on both sides of the fence, and it's a moot point as to which place is best for starters.

Since it's relatively easy to move back and forth, don't agonize about this decision. You might as well follow your instincts. If your tendency is toward a career in advertising, start at an agency. If you're also interested in merchandising and marketing, begin at a company. You can't go wrong either way. Take Mary, for example. She came to New York and headed straight for an ad agency. She started as a secretary on the Revlon account. "I did just about every job there was on that account: secretary, traffic, casting, assistant account executive, and, finally, account exec. I probably would have made supervisor had I stayed; but I knew it was time to try my wings, so I left.

"I took a job as product manager on make-up for a cosmetic company. My advertising background certainly helped me get the job, although it didn't exactly prepare me for what I had to do. But what fun! I worked with all the 'shaded' items sold by the company, which means I wrote and implemented marketing plans, worldwide. So I had to travel all through Europe for my job, which wasn't exactly hard to take. I also helped develop all the new products. It was my job to tell the lab if a lipstick was too brown, or not brown enough, for the next season. It was also my job to decide whether the company should come out with a new 'moist' make-up, or concentrate on pushing the 'sheer' make-up already in the line.

"Now that I think of it, maybe my advertising experience helped me in a subliminal way. I had learned the principles of timing and promotion. I knew how to watch the competition and how to adapt successes on one level of the marketplace to another. What I didn't realize until after I made the move was how much better I like this end of the business. I was happy in advertising; nervous, but happy. I just wasn't fascinated by it. I love marketing, though, and would never switch back." Since we spoke, Mary has joined a very prestigious cosmetic firm as marketing director on "treatment" products. At the moment, she's happily planning how all of us can spend money keeping ourselves young forever.

Slow and steady can be the happiest route to the top. You can tell readily enough if you're going no place in an organization. Just don't be fooled by the inevitable plateaus every career experiences. Those breathers are beneficial, too. They give you much-needed time to refine and practice what you know. Don't be in so much of a hurry for success that you overreach yourself. You'll run the risk of taking on more than you can handle. There are few things as uncomfortable as having to learn, on the job, from the people who work under you.

Another example of the simple switch is to work in different areas of the same overall industry. One of the best training grounds for any career in fashion would be to start with a job on a fashion magazine, get your experience there, and then switch. Many of the top women in the field today are fashion magazine alumnae. As a matter of fact, we could fill a whole book with the success stories of women who began as go-fers on one of the big magazines and then shifted to other areas of the fashion industry. If what you're looking for is to learn about fashion from the ground up, there's no better place than on a magazine. Just by being around the office you'll be exposed to all the elements of the fashion business. As an assistant, you'll learn how to deal with people as well as how to present ideas creatively and successfully. Many a smart assistant has become an editor, earned her pennies every week while making a name for herself, and then parlayed all that expertise into a fabulous career on the outside.

Career Building vs. Job Hopping ⪢

There's been a swing in recent years away from the fluffy, Ivory Tower approach to fashion and the industry is now more down-to-earth than it's ever been. It may be a bit harder today to switch to industry from a magazine, but if fashion experience is what you want, it's still a great place to start. There's something unique about the people who can keep fashion intriguing month after month; it's a world of sophisticated tastes and incredible talent.

One ex-editor we've known for years is now in charge of licensing for a famous French couturier. She handles all the design approvals and business dealings. It's a super job, which enables her to travel all over the world. "What you need to make it in fashion," she told us, "is taste, talent, and guts. You can't be afraid to take risks. Magazine work teaches you to trust your own point of view. That's an invaluable asset in the business. The sad thing is that in order to earn a decent living, you have to move on." Hence, the simple switch. We've met women in just about every area of the fashion establishment who have come from magazines. You'll find them in advertising, public relations, beauty; an inordinate number of successful women *started* on magazines. Sure, times are changing, and it's harder now to make the move; but as the lady said, "In fashion, you've got to take risks!"

However, let's make one thing perfectly clear: we're talking about a simple switch, not a see-saw. Swinging back and forth too often can work negatively against you. To be valuable as a professional, you have to become an expert. It's preferable to build from a broad background, yes, but ultimately it's wise to develop expertise in one area. Flip-flopping from one side to another makes people think you can't decide what you want to do. Keep in mind that while a crossover does provide very tangible benefits (more money, experience from another vantage point, new contacts, a more comprehensive view of the industry), at some point you're going to have to choose one side or the other.

Building Blocks

The building block approach to career planning is a tricky business, mostly because it's potentially dangerous. That is to say, if you can make it work, it's worth a lot; but if you fail, you can wind up no place. Be forewarned, this route is not for neophytes; it's career packaging as high art. It requires careful thought, the ability to project long range, and talent. What we're talking about is combining elements of experience in several industries to build several areas of expertise. The result is a unique and enormously valuable package if you can bring it off; otherwise, you turn out to be the consummate generalist, not really qualified to do much of anything.

Most people don't start out down this path. They start at a company, make a simple switch, and then, instead of remaining with what they know, they accept a third job in a totally new area. Obviously, you can work in various ends of one industry without any grave risk to your professional future. It's only when you switch industries repeatedly that you're skating on thin ice. You begin to increase your "downward potential" with each move.

Some extremely bright and gifted women have proved very successful at using the building blocks approach; others are stymied with a reputation as Jill-of-all-trades, mistress of none. Gayle is a famous glamour-industry woman whose career path went as follows:

magazine—*editor*
ad agency—*fashion director*
department store—*advertising and publicity V.P.*
textile industry—*corporate executive V.P.*
cosmetic company—*prestige-division president*

She's done it all, it would seem, but there's a subtle interlocking at work here. It looks (in retrospect) as if she zigzagged up the ladder. Her ability to straddle the creative and business aspects of industry is most unusual. Top management requires sophisticated business and financial capabilities, for one thing. For another, it takes terrific flair and imagination to make the grade in fashion or retail advertising where one must be able to set a distinct style and project a strong image. Gayle has demonstrated magnificently that she has the talent to handle just about anything. That's why she's been so successful; that's why she's famous.

Not everyone can be Gayle, however. When you consider moving from one industry to another, consider in what way the experience you'll be gaining is pertinent to your previous background. If it's not (unless you hate what you've been doing), think twice. It's important to build a "package" that blends the various elements on your resumé. Are you acquiring expertise? Or are you just drifting all over the lot?

"No one thinks of me when there's a job opening anywhere," Betsy complained. She, too, started on a magazine and then switched to an ad agency. Her third move, to a department store, turned out to be a dead end. A pleasant one, perhaps, but she's bored. "I work for one of the most exciting stores in the country and I go to Europe twice a year on buying trips. But I just don't want to spend the rest of my life in retailing. I really didn't like working for an ad agency enough to go back to that, and I can't earn as much money as I am now on a magazine. I've been here six years and I don't know where to move." Betsy's problem, it seems to us, is that she's not a specialist at anything. In today's business world, and at Betsy's stage of the game, that's a big minus. She's ready for new challenges and undoubtedly could handle them. Unfortunately, her background doesn't indicate any definitive areas of strength.

Gretchen, our producer friend, put it this way, "You have to get to be really good at something. Maybe that's what is meant by the word *professional*. I'd be embarrassed if anyone ever counted up all the places I've worked. First of all, they'd think I was 103 years old. But in production you can move around pretty easily. Staying put is less important than having a reputation as a deliverer. I've had lots of jobs—in television, movies, advertising. But always in production. What matters is that I know my craft and that I can be trusted to bring jobs in on time and within budget." From the point of view of an employer, the difference between Betsy and Gretchen is obvious.

THE QUESTION OF LOYALTY

The fine distinction between being loyal (to your boss, to your company) and passing up a once-in-a-lifetime chance often depends on who's telling the story. Ethics are alive and well in the marketplace. People who forget that fact often find they've made one opportunistic move too many. Maybe this should be etched in stone: you have a responsibility to the people who pay you. There's an even exchange between employer and employee, fair and ample remuneration for the best job that can be done. It may be an unwritten contract, but this understanding should be upheld by both parties. If either defaults, then it's reasonable for steps to be taken. Under the best circumstances loyalty can be expected to work in both directions. You're good to them and they're good to you.

Sometimes, the question of loyalty can prove to be touchy. Karen (who, you may remember, got her first job break via a cup of coffee) had some excellent advice on this subject. She'd been working for the network as producer on a series of specials. The star of the programs had been reluctant to have her on the set, at first. "It was understandable," said Karen. "He thought of me more as a spy for the network than as his producer. By the end of production, however, we'd become fast friends and we've worked together a number of times since then."

We knew that the network had been very pleased with Karen's work on those specials, and we wondered how she'd managed to make star and network both feel as if she was on "their" side. "That's easy," Karen told us, without hesitation. "I'm always loyal to my job. I did what I thought was best for the project. When that meant sticking up for the network's point of view, I did that. Other times, I fought like a steer for the show, no matter how high up in network hierarchy I had to go. I always work hard and I always do my best. They can't hate you for that." To which we say "Amen."

There are two specific points we'd like to emphasize, in regard to loyalty. The first is never to say negative things about your company, your boss, or your co-workers to anyone. This is especially important on an interview. Even if you hate your job, don't say so. If you bad-mouth your current employer to an interviewer, you'll give the impression that someday you may do the same about your next employer. A little restraint will go a long way and serve you well. Business people acknowledge the fact that not everybody sees eye-to-eye, and you'll get your point across well enough if you indicate you have a difference of opinion with management or have a personality clash with someone. Don't go into details and don't place blame. All that's necessary is to state there's a problem and that the details are irrelevant to your skills and accomplishments. If your company or your boss has a bad reputation, your interviewer undoubtedly knows about it and will respect you for not dwelling on the subject. Obviously, you can discuss work problems with friends, but even friends have been known to repeat things, sometimes to people you wouldn't have chosen to confide in.

Confidentiality is topic two. You can't be too careful. Most companies prefer to conduct their business in private, if not in outright secrecy, and leaks can be costly. You might think that your friends or family can't matter. "Who'd my Mother tell?" you might say. No one, probably. The point is that once you tell one person, it's that much easier to tell another. The safest thing is not to discuss office particulars at all, with anyone. When in doubt, don't talk about it. We repeat, you just can't be too careful.

Final thought: It makes sense to sniff around the industry every few years or so, just to make sure your salary has kept up with the going rate. The only way you'll know what you'd be worth elsewhere is to go and find out. That's not disloyalty; that's keeping yourself informed. It doesn't hurt to job hunt for your own edification. No law says you have to take a new job, and you'll learn what's happening outside your company.

EIGHT

❧ *Is It Too Late?*

It's never too late to be happier. We can't tell you how many women we've talked to who have exciting, glamorous careers today (and we don't mean women in the first, sweet blush of youth, either) who were doing something else a few years ago. Women who were married and raising families and decided to get back into the working world. Women who were teachers, social workers, librarians, government employees (even a lawyer or two), who felt they missed their calling. Women who were just bored with their lives and wanted more challenging worlds to conquer. Or women who, by circumstances, were forced back into the mainstream. All of them started new careers and are happier now than they were before.

We also talked to lots of women who preferred the safe harbor of a job they know and love to gripe about. And that's fine, for them. Griping is one of the great national pastimes. We also spoke with lots of happy housewives, who view their lives as full and challenging. And we agree. Having a happy home and healthy children *is* a creative enterprise. One marvelously witty housewife we know, tired of being put down for "doing nothing" while raising three children, started to tell people she "worked for a nonprofit organization in child development." The point is to be satisfied. If staying where you are—be it the job you've got now or at home—makes you happy to get up in the morning, we're in favor of it.

IF YOU WANT TO GO BACK
TO WORK

If you are looking for something more than you have now—excitement, intellectual stimulation, money —it's not too late for a glamour career. Of course, there's a price to be paid (isn't there always?). The inveterate late-show watcher, who used to sleep till ten, will have to change her habits. The dutiful housewife, who always had dinner on the table when her husband came home, may have to reschedule her family a bit. The mother, who always was there when the children came home from school, may have to hire babysitters and may find herself torn by ambivalent feelings. The women who've done it swear that it's worth it, but admonished us to warn you that you're going to have to learn to deal with your guilt feelings.

Guilt is pervasive, so the first step in changing your life seems to be to rid yourself of hang-ups. The meticulous housekeeper must learn to accept a less-than-perfect house. "You can't eat off my floor anymore," one woman told us, "but the money I earn has taken us all to Europe. I had terrible pangs at first, but, you know, I'm beginning to think my husband and kids never cared that our house was spotless. We seem a much closer family now, too, because the time we spend together is so precious." Another woman, noted for her gourmet cooking and elegant parties in a pre-job era, said, "I've had to sacrifice a large part of our social life. I'm just too tired. But we bought a lovely old house in the country for weekends, and we invite friends up there. All we really did, I guess, was to stop spending so much time with acquaintances."

There are compensations, then, for what you're giving up. You make the choice, so you make the adjustments. That's fine, as far as it goes. It's not so easy to control the people around you, particularly families who are used to a certain kind of routine, a certain amount of attention. The old ways die hard. Husbands and children *like* being spoiled. We enjoy catering to our families. It makes us feel needed and unselfish, and that's very gratifying. It's not easy, all of a sudden, to cut loose from that mold because you want to "do" something for yourself. Ergo, guilt. And, often, we're faced with disapproval—from our mothers (who think we should be home, tending to family business), from our husbands or lovers (who think we should keep busy, so long as it doesn't interfere with them, or their comfort, in any way), and from our children, who may indicate they feel deserted.

Somehow, you can still be guilt-riddled even if the reason you're going to work is to augment, or supply, family income. A psychologist friend of ours told us,

"No one makes you feel guilty; only you can make yourself feel guilty." So, steel yourself and begin to deal with it. The transition from what was to what is takes time. Our friend Susan, who works for a specialty shop with several branch stores, told us about "the wrench of separation" she experienced when she decided to go back to work. "You just can't imagine the trauma I went through," she said. "I had never been an overprotective mother, but all I could envision was that the kids were in accidents someplace, falling off their bicycles or something, and I wouldn't be there to rush them to the doctor. Every cold they got, my first year back at work, I was sure was due to my neglect. And if I had to spend the day away, at one of our branch stores, I worried all day."

Realize now that the first thing you have to do before starting work is get your head together. Then, organize your life. Who is going to attend to the marketing, laundry, car pools? How? When? Will dinnertime have to be changed? All the minutiae. Tell your family that you've decided to get a job. Don't ask them. If you ask, even the most supportive family can make you doubt your own mind. "Gee, Mom, I think that's just great. But who'll make lunch for me?" Or, "How will I get to dancing school?" Or, "If you want to work, that's wonderful; I'll just take my suit to the cleaners myself." Your family loves you and they don't mean to make you feel guilty—but. You'll be inconveniencing them, but where is it written that you were born to do *their* errands, be at *their* beck and call, give up *your* fulfillment to spoil them? You'll be amazed how well everyone can function for themselves, how resourcefully everyone can manage. We promise. We're not telling you to ignore your responsibilities. Just realign your priorities.

Wendy, a tall, lithe blonde with three teenaged children, went back to work a year ago. "The children are better than they ever were. That's absolutely no problem at all. What has been a difficult adjustment, not only for me but for every working woman my age that I know, is *time off*. I'm just starting out, but my husband has been working for over twenty years. He's entitled to at least three weeks' vacation a year now, and a variety of days off here and there. I'm not. Sure, I can ask for a little extra time, without pay; but that separates me from the serious workers in the minds of everyone else in the office. For example, I'm supposed to work on the days between Christmas and New Year's. My husband and children want to go skiing. I guess I'll just have to leave them in Vermont and drive up and back. My husband's college reunion is coming up soon. It's a terrific four-day weekend. How can I take time off for that? It's not sick leave. And it looks terrible if I take two days off every time I feel like it."

This is a serious problem; face it now. No matter how time consuming being a housewife or mother can be, your time is your own, flexible. You can make the beds and do your work whenever you choose. Or let it all go, if you choose. But when you make the commitment to a job, your time is divided and scheduled. If you've been up too late the night before, if your throat feels scratchy, if the painter is coming, you still have

to get to the office on time. The shock to the system
and the psyche is tremendous. You're simply not used
to working fifty weeks a year, every day, five days a
week. Even mothers of little children can grab catnaps
now and then. Not when you're working. It will take
time for you to adjust. It requires a personal discipline
you had better be prepared to impose on yourself.

After many years of work, husbands achieve a certain level of seniority, status, and success, no matter
what the job. They'll be entitled to a lot of fringe benefits you won't, yet. No matter how encouraging your
husband may be about your job, he won't be exactly
thrilled about the limitations your time off imposes on
him. After all, he's worked like a dog (presumably) all
these years to reach this point in his career. And now
you can't get away. Work it out now, before things
like trips and reunions come up. It's sticky, but not
insoluble. Part-time employment can be the answer to
this problem for some women. This book is about
starting a career, however, and a part-time first job
that leads anywhere is almost nonexistent. If you have
some creative talent, like writing or illustrating, you
may be able to find some part-time or free-lance situation. Usually, an already acquired reputation is
needed to launch you, so unless you've made a name
for yourself in some field it can prove a difficult row
to hoe. There have been numerous books and magazine articles written recently about how to get into the
professional world on a part-time basis, and it's certainly worth a try.

Of course, people today grow up with a different

attitude about all of these domestic things we've been discussing. So they start at a different place. But women who were raised in a pre-"lib" era have set, preconceived notions—taught them by their mothers —of what a woman should be. It's harder for them to change their life-styles, and just as hard for their families to adjust. One husband we know said, "I'm the same as when we got married. It's you who's changed!" And he's right. So, going to work outside the house (you'll never catch *us* saying housewives don't work!) can create some problems. Usually, they're a matter of logistics, easy enough to iron out with family cooperation. Just solve the problems beforehand.

Even a glamour job, of course, can't be the panacea for all personal/emotional ills. When you take a job you're exchanging one routine for another. But it's a great, big, stimulating world and, although your life may become more complicated, it'll become much more interesting. As one mother we met put it, "I just couldn't stand not talking to anyone over the age of ten all day!"

Women today no longer look only to men to fill their lives. We are very aware that personal happiness is generated from within. Maybe it's because so many of us witnessed our mothers' sense of loss and rootlessness when we flew the nest. In any case, we've learned that nothing is more boring than a steady diet of time on one's hands. Unlike the past, when divorce was a rarity for the well-to-do, thousands of once-married women now find themselves alone, with children to raise and, often, support. For good or for ill, divorce is a fact of everyday life. It's a whole new ball game from any previous generation. One of the results is that women now expect different things from life than before; another is that girls as well as boys grow up assuming they'll participate in the workaday world.

One very close friend of ours explained her reason for going back to work. "I'll never forget how my father, who's a newspaperman, would come home from being with all those fabulous people all day, and say to my mother: 'Don't tell me about the butcher.' Well, my husband doesn't meet fascinating people at work, and he's not particularly interested in day-to-day trivia, either. I admit the house doesn't run as smoothly as it did before I went back to work. But I'm a lot happier now, and my dinner table conversation is a lot more interesting because my days are more interesting."

"Working can be a mixed blessing," a fashion director we met told us. She went back to work when her children were in grade school. "Business takes me to South America twice a year. As a matter of fact, my company is paying for my Spanish lessons at Berlitz. I also take several trips to Europe each year to see the collections. One time, my plane from Rio landed at Kennedy Airport at just about the same time my husband's plane took off for his business trip to Paris. That can be a pain. But I love my work. I'm surrounded by creative people, which is very stimulating. I've made lots of friends and I feel terribly international. No matter where I go—Paris, Milan, London,

Rio—I have friends. And when they come to New York, they visit us. It's a merry-go-round but it's exciting!"

Success stories of reentry women are far too numerous to catalog here. One thing to keep in mind, though, is that people in the business world are fearful that housewives have been out of it too long. Let's face it, the reentry woman has to prove herself. You have to get in, get started. Go to the personnel department of a company you're interested in and take anything. Cut swatches, address envelopes, wrap samples, anything. Take whatever skills you have and apply them. If it means being a bookkeeper or a saleswoman, it doesn't matter. The next job is there to be had, once you're in. If you have tried diligently to find a promising first job with no success, you might consider working as an apprentice, for nothing. In principle, we're against "volunteering" one's services, but it's a tactic to get in the door. Be sure there is a firm understanding of the time limit, however, and that you will be given ample opportunity to display the qualities which would make you a valued, salaried employee. Your boss will see quickly enough how reliable you are, how enthusiastic you are, how valuable you are. Enthusiasm is a particularly important asset, as is the ability to get along with people. These are characteristics in what is called a promotable personality. If you have 'em, you'll move up. Otherwise, you'll just stay there and type. In the working world, there's simply no place for moodiness or temperament.

Earlier in this book, we mentioned the advantages

of using contacts in the process of job hunting. Since the older we get, the more people we meet, reentry women are actually in a better position (in this regard) than some of their younger counterparts. So, be smart. Noise it around, socially, that you're thinking of going back to work. There's no reason to keep it secret, and you never know where or how you'll get a lead. The assistant to one of the top public relations men in the country told us she met her boss at a party. "I nudged him for a year to give me a job. What I really wanted was to work part-time, as an apprentice, to see if I liked it. He told me there was no such thing as part-time in P.R. So, I convinced him to let me work, without pay, for three or four months." She obviously did well, because she went on salary after that. She admits that her hours are crazy and she's always too busy to go out for lunch. But she loves every minute of it. As a matter of fact, we had to interview her on the telephone, in the evening, because she just didn't have the time to see us. Our conversation was cut short when Rex Reed called on her private number. Less than five years ago, she was a suburban housewife. Today, she says, "excitement is an everyday thing."

IF YOU'RE THINKING OF PLAYING SWITCH

One of the toughest problems to solve is whether or not to change careers. Is it too late? Has the boat sailed? Are you better off where you are?

There's no one answer to so complicated and crucial a question. Some women really would rather complain than switch. Other women are genuinely unchallenged, feel they've missed their calling, and dread going to work every day. Women in that position should weigh their options very carefully. If you can live with your job, more or less happily, even though you don't find it exhilarating, then the odds are that you probably shouldn't change. You're just not unhappy enough. There are frustrations and dissatisfactions in every job and you may prefer to stick with the ills you know rather than run to those you can only imagine. If you only hate your job *some* days, changing fields may not be worth the ordeal involved.

On the other hand, you only live once. We believe your day-to-day existence should be as marvelous as you can make it. We're not gamblers, particularly, but sometimes taking a risk is worth the effort. Even though your innermost career ambitions aren't being realized, if you leave, you'll have to sacrifice some degree of status and security in exchange for what you *think* may be out there. But the rewards can be substantial. It's not easy to generalize about the advisability of switching careers, but we'll discuss some of the pros and cons.

If you have a real stake in what you're doing now, it's awkward to picture yourself starting all over again. It's not just the money, although that's not an incidental complication. The major stumbling block facing most women who decide on a career shift seems to be ego. It's the insecurity of having to face friends and acquaintances as a secretary or an assistant again, rather than being someone who's "accomplished something," with a more or less impressive title to prove it. This is a perfectly understandable reaction, so don't be embarrassed to admit it to yourself. Our advice would be to devise something acceptable to say when you're asked what you do: "I've just changed fields and am trying to break into . . ." for example. It's the truth, yet at the same time cushions your ego. As for having to go back to a menial job again, you'll be learning a new field, and that's a great compensation.

Financial considerations can't be ignored, of course. The success you've earned in a profession you don't love, however, is unlikely to be greater than anything you might achieve in one you do. So a salary cut is a temporary thing. You may have to take a few giant steps backward but it's not forever; and you may not have to go as far back as you might think. Your present status indicates how capable and efficient you are; there's no reason why you can't translate these assets into terms relevant to a new career. The obvious drawback to a decrease in income is that you'll have to reorganize your personal finances. The key question is how long you can manage on what you'll be making. It will be easier for you if you view this change in salary as an investment in your future—an investment with a big payoff not only in money, but in terms of personal gratification.

No matter what you're currently doing, if you've been doing it for any length of time, you know what it is to get up every morning and *do* satisfactorily what is expected and required. That goes a long way with prospective employers. You're also evidencing enormous self-assurance and commitment by your willingness to start again in a new direction.

If you think we're encouraging you to change careers, we are, if you're not happy. If you're bored and in a rut or feel you'll never realize your potential in the field you're in, change. If you figure you'll be doing the exact same thing five years from now, why stay? The problems you'll face in a new career will be challenging and you do stand to make big gains. Don't make any move without careful planning, and be sure that the job you take can lead in the direction you want. Then do it.

Some women are lucky enough to back into new careers. Sue, a vibrant woman with two school-age children, is in charge of "print" and "children" at a very successful theatrical agency. She started working there two days a week as a bookkeeper. What began as a part-time situation evolved into a full-time, important career. She was in the right place at the right time, with all the right abilities. Think about it. Maybe you can find a job using your present background in an industry more exciting to you; as we've said, once you're in, opportunities invariably follow. If you demonstrate your ability and eagerness to assume more responsibility, you'll move up.

At the same time, it's important not to overlook what you're giving up. Very few jobs offer vacations like those in the teaching profession. How much would you miss the holidays and summers off? Don't undersell what that means in your life. On the other hand, just because your father told you that a teaching certificate was the best insurance you could have doesn't mean you're obligated to spend the rest of your life teaching, if you don't want to. Whatever talents you have can be put to good use elsewhere. Don't permit yourself to be nailed in where you don't want to be. When we met Lisa, she had been a government lawyer for ten years, which she liked all right. What she *loves* is clothes. Shopping is her idea of heaven. She can tell who designed what across a crowded room. She should have been a buyer, or in some area of fashion, and she knew it. It was a dilemma. Her job paid a substantial salary; her fringe benefits were fantastic; she was respected in her profession. But she could also have been a lot happier every day. When Lisa asked us what we thought three years ago, we told her the same thing we'd counsel any of the women we meet in similar circumstances: switch. Today she's managing the couture department of a small specialty store. She's still not earning what she had been when she made the move but she's confident that she will surpass it, and she's much, much happier.

NINE

❧ *Words to the Wise*

You need to know certain things to survive in the world of corporate intrigue; it's advice your mother never gave you. The working world can be a tough, dog-eat-dog jungle and it's not always easy to keep your own integrity intact. You'll be happier in the long run, though, if you do. Don't let yourself be sucked into the maelstrom of petty scheming and underhanded behavior; just because someone else fights dirty doesn't mean you should. After a while, you'll be able to tell the dirty dealers without a score-card. At this point, we think some words to the wise might prove extremely helpful. We don't mean to disillusion you, or throw cold water on your enthusiasm, but a dash of icy realism will stand you in good stead.

THE TEN COMMANDMENTS OF OFFICE SURVIVAL

There are no set rules for office politics because protocol varies from company to company. The guidelines change as your status changes. Your smartest move is to steer clear of office politics until you know the ropes. Most offices operate in layers of authority and it's hard to know the infighters without experience. Political maneuvering is a dangerous business at any level. Remain neutral until you're certain you know what you're doing, and you're in a position to gain *significantly;* even then, be very careful.

If you keep in mind that smart office politics are really an extension of old-fashioned good manners, you'll stay out of trouble. Follow our suggestions and you won't strike out, at least not before you've had your chance at bat.

1.   *Avoid politics.* Stay as far away from office intrigue as you can. Never say anything you wouldn't want repeated to a colleague's face because everything you do say can, and will, be used against you. Never underestimate the guile of a "friend."

2.   *Observe hierarchy always.* There is no exception to this rule. All complaints, suggestions, questions, and so on should be taken to the person directly above you. Never go over anyone's head. Memos should be addressed to your counterpart in another department, with copies to those higher up. If in doubt, ask who should receive copies. You'll appear inefficient or thoughtless if you leave someone out, particularly lower-echelon people.

3.   *Give credit where credit is due. Don't place blame.* These two are different sides of the same coin.

You never diminish yourself by praising others. You'll appear much more intelligent and interested in the good of the company, as a matter of fact, if you make sure that credit for a good idea goes to those who deserve it. It's not a bad way to make friends, either. This doesn't mean that someone else won't take credit due you for your good suggestions. When that happens, there's not much you can do. It will reflect badly on you if you tattle, and, anyway, people catch on to that kind of thing sooner than later.

Placing blame also never accomplishes much of anything. Your boss is far more concerned with how to solve the problem in the fastest, least expensive way. Do that, and you'll come out ahead. You'll also avoid being in the uncomfortable position of pointing an accusing finger and may make a friend in the process. It's do-unto-others, because when you goof the last thing you'd want is someone shining a spotlight on your mistake. When you do blunder, admit it. No matter how costly, stupid, inexcusable, admit it yourself. Even if it looks like there's a chance you'll never be found out. Go straight to your boss. It's a very disarming tactic for getting off the hook. Try to have a plausible excuse, and a solution. *Mea culpa* is the best, most honest way out of hot water, as long as it doesn't become a habit. Save tears, however, for the ladies' room. Admit your error, make amends, and get on with your work.

4. *Make friends.* For something that sounds so simple you'd be amazed how often people overlook

the advantage of making friends. We don't mean to court people you dislike or become a flatterer. Just be nice like Mama always said you should. Think about the other person's feelings and remember the little things that are important to them. Ask how a sick child is feeling, for instance, or how the dinner party went. Show equal concern for those "below" you as those above. Remember, an enemy will never help you. A "friend" may not either, but at least there you've got a fighting chance.

5. *Handle problems in a straightforward manner.* The best way to approach misunderstandings is to go directly to the person involved and talk it out. Maybe you were misinterpreted or unwittingly offended somebody. Say you're sorry. Some people choke on those words, which is a shame. It's easy to apologize and clear the air. If you've been hurt, give the other person room to make amends. The point is to eliminate tension and undercurrents where and when you can. Be as genuine and humane a person as you know how. Your treatment of others will be reflected in their treatment of you.

6. *Listen.* You'll get your chance to be heard; let someone else talk, too. Listening is not the same thing as waiting for your chance to speak. Talking is only one-half of communication; the other half is attending to what's been said. Think before you say something and hear the answer. When you reply, respond to the other person's comment. Most people

are terrible listeners. If you really keep your ears open, you'll learn a lot (sometimes from the most unexpected sources).

7. *Be trustworthy.* When you say you'll do it, do it. Always follow through, and don't leave anyone in the lurch. If plans change, alert everyone and anyone who could possibly be affected. No matter how rushed you are, take the extra minute to think about who should know whatever it is, and make sure they're told. There's nothing more awful than not knowing something that affects you or your department. Only you yourself can build a reputation for reliability. It takes time, but it's worth it, and it's the little things that can make it or break it.

8. *Treat everyone with equal respect.* There is absolutely no excuse for not following this rule with everyone—above you, below you, regardless of age or position.

9. *Protect yourself.* Without seeming fanatic, confirm all agreements in writing. Some version of what is colloquially known as the "cover your ass" memo exists in every business. Just because you're trustworthy and above blame-placing doesn't mean the other guy is. A memo that begins, "This is to confirm our agreement," can and will become your best friend. It's called being "buttoned up," and that's just what you want to be.

10. *Nice guys don't finish last.* Dumb guys and doormats do. Just because you're nice to everyone doesn't mean you shouldn't stand up for what you believe in. Don't be afraid to speak your mind or voice an unpopular opinion. Never be controversial or argumentative just for the sake of it, but don't avoid delicate issues, either. Only egomaniacs need to be surrounded by "yes men." Reputations are often made by people who are willing to stand up and be counted. You'll be respected for saying what you honestly think, even if you're overruled. In the final analysis, it's the boss's responsibility to make the decision. It's your job to abide by and, perhaps, implement what is decided. Be true to yourself and take your victories and defeats with equal grace.

FAIR PLAY IS NOT THE ONLY GAME IN TOWN

Sad to say, not everyone in business follows the Golden Rule. Now that we've told you how to play the game, we have to warn you that ambition can do strange things to the nicest seeming people. Someone who wouldn't steal a dime, for instance, is capable of plagiarizing your copy. It always comes as a shock, because we never really expect bad behavior from anyone. While you will meet many decent, honorable people, you'll also encounter the rotters. You won't be hurt as badly if you're aware of this fact from the outset.

Even the rosy glamour world has thorns. Amidst the people who play by the rules are those who specialize in making their own as they go along. It may get them nowhere in the long run, but you have to deal with them in the present. It pays to be cautious. A close associate may connive behind your back to get a promotion ahead of you, or someone may "forget" to tell you about a crucial meeting. The ambitious, undermining personality can devise all sorts of chicanery. The worst of it is these things always seem to happen when we least expect them. The only way to handle the situation is to keep your indignation to yourself. Don't discuss it with everyone in the office. As we said in the "Ten Commandments," it's degrading to you to tattle. The offender is well aware of that fact and is counting on it; that's part of the strategy. Just let the episode pass. You know what kind of person the culprit is and can act accordingly. If it's a serious enough offense, you can confront the person, once you've calmed down. If you're dealing with an inveterate dirty trickster, however, you may not get too far. Don't get involved in a vendetta; trying to get even never pays off. If the situation is chronic and you can't make any headway talking to the guilty one, you have the option of discussing the problem with your immediate superior. Explain quietly and ask for help. If your boss is the one in question, you're in big trouble. Only you can judge, at the time, if the dilemma is worth the waves you'll make if you talk to anyone about it. If it's any consolation, tricksters trap themselves eventually and get their comeuppance. We've known people who've found opportunities for revenge. They say they can live with the consequences, if any, and that it's worth it. We think there's something to be said for the satisfaction of having the goods on someone and not using it; it's called one-upmanship.

BITS AND PIECES

There are extraneous pieces of advice which come out in conversations sometimes, but which aren't really of monumental importance. All the same, this information may come in handy for you. We're going to run through it quickly, in no particular order.

What to Tell Your Mother

Not very much. The same goes for well-meaning friends, husbands, lovers, and roommates. Our lives are filled with people who are absolutely authoritative about what we should do next and what we should have replied when so-and-so said such-and-such. Tell everyone that your job is fine. If the word secretary doesn't suit your mother's image of you, say you're an assistant. She's probably worried about how to tell her friends that her Phi Beta Kappa daughter is taking dictation, not giving it. It's a case of packaging. Life will run much more smoothly for you if you tell your family how much you like your job, even if you have reservations. There's nothing more frustrating after an aggravating day than having to rehash the whole thing over dinner or on the phone. It's going to take the world a little while to discover you, and what you don't need is people clucking over you until it happens. Give your mother some amusing anecdotes to feed her friends and save in-depth career analysis for people who are best equipped to advise you.

Keep a Private Business File

As we said earlier, you can't remember everything. You'll save yourself a lot of work and digging through piles of papers if you keep a general business file at home. Save anything that is pertinent to your business. You can always clean out the file later, when you're more experienced and better able to judge what's necessary to keep. Here are some suggestions of things you'll be happy you didn't throw away:

Articles: Any magazine or newspaper articles about your industry. Read them and file. You never know when you or your boss will have to write a report; that article you vaguely recall having read someplace will be right at your fingertips.

Office memos: Any correspondence which might provide you with a good format to copy. Most businesses require periodic use of specific documents and interoffice correspondence, such as marketing plans, personnel evaluations, status reports, year-end summaries. Start saving specimens now against the time you'll be asked to handle them.

Letters: Xerox any particularly good congratulatory notes or memos that come into your office; do the same for any angry letters (they're even harder to write). When you're called on to send good wishes for someone's promotion, or are asked to draft a scold-someone memo, you'll have an idea of how to go about it.

This private file belongs at home, not in the office. Should you change jobs for some reason, it would be terribly awkward to be seen leaving with a bulky file under your arm. Weed out the file frequently, because the bigger it is, the more cumbersome it is to use. Be sure to include your own good letters and memos in the file, too; we forget our own deathless prose as easily as that of others.

Keep a Chronological File

A "chron" file is a daily file of everything you type, for yourself or your boss. One of those jumbo three-ring notebooks is perfect for this purpose. Some offices have other filing systems and, by all means, adhere to their requirements, but use this one in addition. We tend to remember things in sequence of time ("I know we sent a memo to Mr. X about something after such-and-such took place"), not necessarily by subject matter. Experience has proved that we use our chron file more than any other.

Final Thoughts

Never discuss your job or any of your co-workers in public places. There was a slogan during World War II that stated "the walls have ears." You never know who will overhear what you're saying in a restaurant or supermarket or the ladies' room. We'll spare you the tales of woe we've heard. Trust us and speak your private thoughts in private places.

Keep your sense of humor and don't take everything too seriously. Beginners often view every decision as a crisis, every mistake as fatal. Lighten it up a little. A mistake isn't the end of the world. There will always be another chance if you botch something up. Taking the hard knocks in stride is a sign of professional maturity. Keep your perspective.

Learn to say "I'm wrong" and "I don't know." That's very hard for some of us, but important nonetheless. No one can know everything and no one can be right all the time. It's much better to ask than to guess.

Trust your own opinion. Don't let other people's attitudes affect your judgment. Give yourself time to draw your own conclusions about people, issues, pros and cons. New people at work are frequently bombarded by well-intentioned advisers on who is and isn't liked in the office. Give yourself a chance to make up your own mind.

TEN

🔌 *Sex and the Office*

A whole book could be written on this subject alone. We're not going to do that, but we feel obligated to include some commentary on sex and the office. In any arena where men and women meet, there can be chemistry. Certainly in an office situation, where people work together closely on a daily basis, the possibilities are even greater. We are not interested in launching into a discussion of moral or ethical values. People are people, our Puritan forebears notwithstanding, and will behave as such. Our remarks here are made from a pragmatic point of view in terms of your career.

Sex and the office? To put it succinctly, don't. There's no way to come out ahead, somehow, when you mix business and sex. Despite the propaganda of all the old Rosalind Russell movies of the forties (she always wound up with Melvyn Douglas or Brian Aherne), it too often doesn't work out. Someone will get hurt and often careers can take a battering, too. From a completely practical standpoint, your social life should be separate from your career. You'll avoid being the subject of gossip, for one thing. It's your private life, after all, no one else's.

We realize that one of the benefits of a career in the glamour industries—especially for those of you who are unattached—is the opportunity to meet some of the most glamorous men in the world. That's true. Just choose from the eligibles not in your immediate sphere of operations. And never (God forbid!) your client. It's possible, of course, that the man-for-you will turn up in your office, and you'll just know that this man can mean more to you than any job. Our best advice would be to continue your relationship with him, and start job hunting. Or ask him to. Changing a job before or in the earliest stages of a grand romance is infinitely preferable to changing later (when, alas, it's over). Let's face it, if he's not worth shifting jobs for now, he certainly won't seem worth it later; and, somehow, affairs at work inevitably lead to job changes. Look, we believe in happily-ever-after, too; it's just that we also believe in the practicality of that old working-couple's motto: two people who head home together in the evening should go to different addresses in the morning.

In today's corporate world, companies can be big places with many departments and divisions. It's possible that you'll encounter somebody sensational from another division. He's fair game, as long as he's not in a strong enough position in the company to have you fired or transferred when he decides he'd rather not see your cheerful—or tear-stained—face any longer. By definition, affairs have a beginning, a middle, and an end; most of us, male and female alike, don't relish the idea of running into an ex-inamorata every morning of every day at work. Who can predict how even the most glorious, blissful affair will end? Maybe he'll be ready to be true forever and you'll meet someone else. His pride may be so wounded that he'll want to hurt you back. Don't involve yourself with someone who has the power to do you in!

We don't really mean to sound cynical; it just happens very often. Sunny, the blonde blockbuster publicity director of a large department store, corroborated what we've been telling you, sad to say. "In principle, I don't believe in mixing business with pleasure," Sunny told us. "It can only cause trouble. I did get involved with someone sort of tangentially associated with my business, though. He was one of my key suppliers. A super guy to do business with, and everything he did for us was terrific. His work made *me* look good, if you know what I mean. Well, after several years of friendly lunches and occasional drinks after work, we sort of backed into a "thing" together. I knew that mixing my social life with my business life wasn't the greatest idea in the world, but I figured *I* was his client, let *him* worry. What a mistake. When I got to know him better, away from business, I realized there was less to him than met the eye. So I decided to cool it. You know what? It cost me my best supplier. More than that, I found my authority and status at the office had been undermined by his big mouth. He was so hurt that he talked to everybody. We had lots of friends in common, both business and social, after all the years we'd known each other, and he went crying to all of them for advice and consolation. Half my office knew the most private details of my personal life."

As we said, it's a bummer. There's always a chance that your private life will go public. It's just better if that public excludes the people you work with. (P.S. Sunny eventually changed stores. One of her reasons, she admitted, was to put an end, finally, to what had become a most unpleasant situation.)

We would hate you to eliminate from your list of eligibles all men who are somehow connected to your work. Just be very selective and discreet, and keep in mind that the further removed from your day-to-day work life the man is, the less risky—businesswise—the relationship will be.

Having warned you to be leery of involvement with men indirectly connected to your job, you must realize that it's absolutely playing with dynamite to form a liaison with a close professional colleague. No matter how tempting, don't do it. Unless, as we discussed before, one of you is prepared to change jobs. A gal we know in public relations, who should have known better, summed up her broken romance with her boss this way: "Losing a lover wasn't the worst of it. I lost my most important ally in the office as well." What happened was that the boss was so eager to squelch the gossip and rumors in the office that he bent over backwards to seem unbiased. He stopped going to bat for her when she most needed his support. He'd been a great person to work for before the romance; afterward, he avoided her at all cost. Her solution: she got another job.

The closer to your job the man in your life is, the more likely it is that your affair will become public property. When one of us worked at an ad agency on Third Avenue, our office window looked out on a very modern, mostly glass building. Late Friday afternoons one whole summer, all the tenants in our building rushed to their windows with binoculars. It's surprising the building didn't tilt. Across the way, there was one lighted office. By Labor Day, the whole street knew who was in that office and exactly what they were doing. It may be hard to believe, but it's a true story. We feel sure we don't have to point a moral to that tale.

No discussion of sex and the office is complete without mention of one of the greatest traps in any career: married men. The fact of the matter is that most married men do *not* leave their wives. Some do, yes; most don't. When you hook up with a married man, you're courting disaster. Without even going into the loneliness of weekends and holidays, which is a depressing certainty, you are endlessly in danger of being "found out," which limits where and how such a romance can flourish. In addition, your career can be in jeopardy. Most married men are just "flexing their muscles" to see if the old charm still works or, maybe, they're looking for a little extracurricular activity. Very few men are willing to risk their homes, children, or careers on what is really playtime for them. *You* shouldn't be willing to risk your career for frivolous reasons, either.

If your feelings for a married man are serious, you're in more hot water than we can handle here. The best thing to do would be to avoid the situation in the first place. Concentrate on unattached men, preferably unconnected with your job.

If you're a married woman who finds herself attracted to a man in the office, you've got a whole other problem. We're told that it's not easy to juggle home, husband, children, and a job. If you're enough of a superwoman to manage all that, plus a supplementary relationship, we'd like you to tell us how you do it.

No matter how you slice it, the truth of it is that sex in the office is no way to go. We have yet to hear of a woman whose personal life or career benefited on any level, for any length of time, from a juxtaposition of her business life and her love life. We can't convince ourselves that you'll be the exception. Do yourself a favor and make your mind up in advance to avoid this particular death trap. We don't know where those stories of sleeping one's way to the top got started—not by a woman, in any case.

ELEVEN

❧ *Business Basics*

Ignorance, which isn't bliss to our way of think-ing, can lead to many mistakes early in your career. Unless you've had prior work experience, there's no way to know what people do, day to day, in a job. That in turn makes it most difficult to evaluate any job offers you may receive. How can you know if you want the job, or if it's suited to you, if you have no idea about office routine? Or where that job fits into that company's scheme of things? You really can't. An interviewer can answer certain questions, of course, and some time in the library doing a little preliminary research can answer others. You really need to know something about business in general, too. This chap-ter will outline the most elementary business basics and give an overall picture of the industries we've been discussing.

In each of our industry summaries, we've tried to indicate the general climate vis-à-vis women. It would be nice were we able to state that the situation is get-ting better and better. Unfortunately, this is not the case. A recent article in the *New York Times,* quoting a Labor Department report titled "The Earnings Gap Between Men and Women" states: ". . . the difference between the annual earnings of the average man and the average woman rose more than threefold, from $1,533 in 1955 to $5,063 in 1974." The report goes on to say ". . . much of the male–female differential remains unexplained," and the *Times* adds, "and probably reflects discrimination."

All we can say is that we believe things will change. More job opportunities are available to women now than in the past, and we're hopeful that adjustments in the pay scale will follow. It's at least a good sign that this kind of prejudice is finally being examined and given serious publicity.

BUSINESS VERSUS CREATIVE

We've divided the glamour industries into "business" and "creative" jobs for the sake of simplicity. Obviously, nothing is quite that black and white. Creative people need sound business judgment and successful people on the business side should be able to think creatively. From an organizational standpoint, however, the two functions are separate. In the course of your working lifetime, you'll undoubtedly find exceptions to what is essentially an arbitrary division; this is merely the form we've chosen for easy clarity. For our purposes, the distinction between these two facets can indicate where a particular job might fit into a company's operation and how it will mesh with your talents and aspirations.

There are people who write books, for example, and people who decide which books to publish. There are people who create ads, and people who decide at which market to aim them. There are dress designers and business minds who decide how to price those dresses, how many to manufacture, and so on. For every person who's paid to dream up a new TV series, there's someone out knocking on sponsors' doors trying to get the advertising dollars to support it. In other words, there's a product and a market. Some people create the product (the book, the ad, the dress, the series) and some people sell it (decide which product to sell, to whom, for how much, and where). The service industries, such as advertising and public relations, have several layers of products and markets: their client's product (soap) and their own product (the ad to sell the soap), but the principle is the same. As we outline the general structure of each of the glamour industries, we'll indicate the "creative" and "business" jobs where we think it's helpful. In the sections on movies and broadcasting, we put little emphasis on this; these fields are hard to break into and the jobs are in such demand that we think landing almost any first job in them is a great coup.

FASHION

To many women, if you can't wear it, it's not worth worrying about. A love of fashion is in their blood and they know, very early on, that they want to do something that is involved with clothes. The doors to the fashion world have always been open to women, happily enough, and there are plenty of career opportunities for women of many different talents. Over one million people work in the manufacturing end of the industry alone. The first question to ask yourself, then, is which part of the business interests you. Most fashion jobs are to be found either in manufacturing or retailing. We've covered other related areas, such as working for the fashion press on a paper or magazine; here we'll outline the wonderful business of making the clothes and accessories, and selling them.

Manufacturing

The most glamorous creative job in manufacturing, of course, is designing. Apart from designing clothes, accessories are a whole field unto themselves; think about shoes, handbags, jewelry, scarves, belts. The top designers are involved in a number of markets that often include furs, accessories, active sportswear, home furnishings, luggage, and more. These superstars really act as editors and stylists and usually have several fine designers working for them, each with her/his assistants. This is big business involving big dollars, even though we categorize it as "creative." The name designer inspires the direction of the collection, edits the designs, and makes the final decisions, as well as providing the status and authority to attract affluent consumers.

The long, hard road to the top begins with the job of assistant. There used to be an apprentice system for budding designers; they'd go to Paris and work in the couture houses, starting at the bottom and really learning their craft. Paris is less influential today than ever before and apprenticeships are a thing of the past. It's not easy to get a job today, even as an assistant to an assistant, without a specialized educational background. Three of the best-known schools, all in New York, are Pratt Institute, the Fashion Institute of Technology, and Parsons School of Design. Even with a diploma from one of them, your first job will undoubtedly entail something like draping fabrics or making sample patterns. Other creative jobs can be found in the fabric and fiber houses, which employ their own stylists and designers to work out color forecasts (to be translated into the material that is then sold to clothing manufacturers).

Business jobs in manufacturing are less glamorous than in other industries because of the pressure. Most of them have to do with forecasting and sales. Textile firms, on the other hand, offer more diverse and challenging business careers in marketing, merchandising, and promotion. If you've assessed yourself as a business person and want to work in fashion, head for New York and try for a job in the marketing, merchandising, or promotion departments of one of the big fiber or fabric houses.

Seventh Avenue, the scene of New York's fashion

action, is the least glamorous looking place you've ever seen. If you've never seen the garment center (which includes Broadway, but is referred to as Seventh Avenue), you're in for a shock. The crowded streets, jammed with pushcarts carrying racks of clothes, give no hint of the fabulous world hidden inside those tall buildings. There are sizable manufacturing centers in Los Angeles, Chicago, Miami, Dallas, and San Francisco, but New York is where you'll find most of the jobs. Incidentally, a friend of ours who's wise to the ways of Seventh Avenue after years in the business gave us an insider's tip for job hunters. Ask the doorman and elevator starters in the buildings in the garment district about job openings. Strange as it may sound, these men know who's looking for what in their buildings. You may just hit upon something that way.

While it's true that working on Seventh Avenue itself is no picnic, there's plenty of glamour at the top of the fashion world. Successful designers travel to Europe, sometimes several times a year. Top designers, whose names are on their own labels, relax over two-hour lunches at elegant restaurants like Orsini's and Le Grenouille. They deserve these luxuries because fashion is a pressure business. Firms open and close so fast it's hard to keep them straight. You're considered only as good as your last season, and designers' names come and go, although the best of them manage to relocate. Despite the tension, people in the fashion world couldn't work anywhere else. As we said, it's in the blood.

For more information:

The Fashion Group
9 Rockefeller Plaza
New York, New York   10020

Fashion Institute of Technology
State University of New York
222 West 27th Street
New York, New York   10001

Retailing

A career in retailing is heaven for someone who loves to shop. It's one of the easiest fields to get into because there are fine department stores and specialty shops all across the country. It's also one of the hardest fields to succeed in. Our advice would be to start in a large store, which can be done almost anywhere in the country. This is one career where you don't have to begin as a secretary, at least not if you want to be a buyer. A department-store buyer is as glamorous a career as there is, if you have what it takes (and it takes a lot). We think buyers have the most creative "business" job there is, because the job requires such versatility. A buyer must have a facility with numbers and the ability to manage the business of her own department; in addition, a buyer needs an instinctive flair that enables her to spot a trend and know how to make it work for her market. The most successful buyers work closely with their resources to create merchandise that's right for their particular departments. Buyers spend much of their time shopping the various world markets (which means traveling to all kinds of marvelous places). So far, it may sound like fun and games, but buyers operate under tremendous pressure. They're held responsible for their department's sales, in a business which measures each day's sales against those for the same day the year before. The buyers we interviewed said they had gotten used to the pressure and found the job enormously rewarding. When we asked why, the answer invariably revolved around the fun of working directly with the designers and seeing their own ideas incorporated. For those of you with wanderlust, being a buyer is ideal. Foreign markets are critical today, and the big stores send buyers not only to Europe but to Japan and South America and any other far-flung spot on the globe you can name. Depending on what department of the store you're buying for, you might make numerous trips abroad each year. If your store is based in a smallish city, you can expect to make periodic trips to New York as well as the other fashion centers in the country. These are all business trips, of course, which can mean long hours and aching feet, not to mention working nights and weekends. The competition is fierce, so you can't just relax and enjoy the scenery. The salaries are good, although in direct proportion to the size of your department and the sales record you achieve.

A liberal arts degree will get you into most stores'

training programs, and an MBA is even better; that will put you in line to take advantage of very special store opportunities. Specialized fashion, merchandising, or retailing courses will round out your background and put you that much farther ahead of others after the same job.

Other interesting careers are available in retailing, aside from buying. Most stores have fashion coordinators, whose job is to integrate the merchandise of various departments to present a unified "fashion message" to the consumer. Large stores also have advertising and promotion departments, with an assortment of "creative" and "business" jobs. For those of you with artistic backgrounds, in-store and window display might be an area to investigate.

There is a whole "business" side to retailing that many people don't even think about, or know exists, called store operations. That's the behind-the-scenes process of actually running the store. Large stores with several branches often have separate departments for systems analysis, market and consumer research, and planning and research for new store site locations (which obviously involves traveling). Some stores are beginning to institute a very new department for retailing research. Working in store operations gives you an overview of the store, so you can see how all the departments interconnect, rather than restricting you (as in the case of a buyer) to one small area. To help you break into this facet of retailing, an MBA is helpful, but not essential. Or you can try to get into one of the store's advanced training programs.

BEAUTY

People mistakenly overlook the beauty business in discussions of glamour careers. Beauty is a billion-dollar industry with a multitude of fascinating and highly paid job opportunities. It's an ideal area for women because so many of them, even in the chauvinistic past, have been able to establish brilliant careers in it. Beauty encompasses the pizazz of its first cousin, fashion, and the challenge of big business.

The four main job areas to consider are marketing, sales, product, and creative services. The first two fall into our arbitrary "business" category; the latter two are, loosely, "creative." There are terrific job possibilities in marketing and sales but, as in the rest of the world, the changing times have affected the complexion (sorry) of the industry. In years gone by, the marketing approach was arrived at, more or less, by the "seat of the pants." That is to say, decisions were made as much on *feel* and instinct as on solid research. Industry giants like Charles Revson and Helena Rubinstein, at the helm of their own companies, could decide major issues through instinct. Today, most of the big companies have been bought by larger corporations (with Revlon and Estée Lauder the notable exceptions) and the days of strong individual dominance are over. The very personal influence in the beauty business has been replaced by a corporate mentality. The Colgate-Palmolive people (Rubinstein's parent company) and the Eli Lillys (Elizabeth Arden) hardly run things by the "seat of their pants." Many industry veterans view the passing of the old guard with sadness; others believe it's the only possible way for the business to keep pace with the times. Whether things were better then or not doesn't matter really. The industry is what it is now, and that's what's important to us in terms of careers for today's women.

You'll find it easier to get into marketing if you have an MBA. Breaking into that field is difficult without a graduate degree; it's not impossible to go up through the ranks, it's just harder. For those of you without superior academic credentials, or for women thinking of going back to work who are unable, or unwilling, to move, sales may prove to be the avenue to pursue. Selling behind a department store's cosmetic counter, as a beauty company demonstrator, opens the door to advancement more quickly than most other easy-to-begin careers. Good demonstrators are in position to be promoted to counter managers and, sometimes, to promotional representatives for the company. Promotional reps do the traveling. As for outside sales jobs, selling the line into retail outlets (where the better money is), they're still mostly held by men. This may vary slightly from one company to another, but it's primarily masculine territory. Scandalous but true. What makes it worse is that the beauty industry derives its livelihood *from* women. Our only advice would be to write to any company that interests you and ask what opportunities are available.

We've grouped product and creative services together for the sake of convenience. In fact, product really stands by itself. Product people perfect formulas and shades and devise innovative product concepts. A good eye for color and patience are essential. A background in chemistry isn't exactly required, but would be very helpful. The job is a combination of creativity and business savvy with strong scientific overtones.

Nancy, a top product specialist, told us she always knew that beauty products fascinated her. "At age ten, I was giving facials to my friends. I made my own formula out of Babo mixed with lemon juice and nobody suffered any ill effects that I know of." She's gotten more sophisticated in her thinking, but even then the instinct was there.

Creative services include advertising, sales promotion, public relations, merchandising, and packaging design. Cosmetic houses do an enormous amount of promotion (all those samples you get with purchases, for example) and most companies produce their own promotional literature. Packaging design, as you can well imagine, is terribly important in the beauty business. As a matter of fact, some of the top creative people in the business graduated from packaging departments. The whole area of creative services has terrific possibilities.

As we said, beauty jobs pay extremely well. We mean it; salaries are some of the highest of any of the glamour industries. Nancy, our facial-giving friend, is a good example of how fast and far you can go in the beauty business if you've got what it takes. You don't need to see Nancy's Phi Beta Kappa key to know how smart she is; you can see it in her eyes. You don't have to spend much time with her to be enchanted by her unique turn of mind and slightly tilted sense of humor. She's an absolute delight.

"I began as a writer," Nancy said. "I worked in P.R. and on magazines for twelve years before I realized that I was just an okay writer, not a great one. I know that so-so writers can get plenty of jobs, but they don't earn lots of money. Now money may be a dirty word to some people, but not to me. I think it's important. I work very hard and want to get paid what I think I'm worth. So, I decided to try the beauty field. It's known to pay well and I certainly have a natural flair for beauty products. I was 33 and earning $10,000 a year when I switched careers. In nine years, I was making over $50,000 a year."

Obviously, you have to be sensational to skyrocket like that, but there aren't many industries where you get the chance to move up that quickly. Despite her talent and impressive salary, Nancy admitted she'd been held back because she's a woman. "It wasn't until I got my last job that I finally made V.P. A man would have gotten the title to match the responsibility much sooner. This business has a lot to offer women—in middle management. It's still men who pull the strings at the top."

Even so, the careers and the money for women are available in the beauty industry. The challenge and diversity are there, and so are the glamour and the excitement. And think of all those free samples.

For more information:

Cosmetic Career Women, Inc.
614 West 51st Street
New York, New York   10019

PUBLISHING

Publishing is the ivory tower of the glamour
world. The atmosphere is intellectual and literate, as
you might expect. Authors and editors consummate
sizable deals on the phone or with nothing more than
a "gentleman's handshake." There is something won-
derfully old-fashioned about publishing, despite the
fact that most of today's houses are owned by major
conglomerates (or are in direct competition with
them). In the new big-business climate of publishing
today, authors are more demanding and editors more
businesslike than ever before because publishing
houses are ready to pay big money, up front, for properties they believe will reap sizable commercial returns.
There are differences in careers in book, magazine, and
newspaper publishing, so we'll treat them separately.

Book Publishing

If you love to read and enjoy endless rounds of
cocktail parties, a career in book publishing may be
perfect for you. Most of the glamour jobs are editorial
ones, although there are such tangential areas within

each publishing house as sales promotion, advertising, publicity, subsidiary rights, graphic design (often a good cover can *make* a book), and the like. Top-notch authors and their agents also lead glamorous lives, but those careers are harder to categorize. If you want to be an author you have to write; we can't help you there. Top literary agents are few and far between and many of them are lawyers; if you aspire to that, you can try to land a job in an agent's office but you have to know that you'll have an edge with a law degree.

Most women who are eager for a career in book publishing want to be editors. The best editors are able to balance shrewd business ability with creative talent. To achieve major success, an editor must have a commercial sixth sense. She's got to have the foresight to spot a big winner, then have the business acumen to get the property for her house. This means bidding for the manuscript and negotiating a deal that's satisfactory to the agent (and the author) that will still be profitable for the house. Editors spend a lot of their time reading manuscripts, scouting for new material, and editing the properties they buy. Frequently, an editor puts a package together; that is, she'll create an idea for a book and then entice the right author into writing it. The work in itself is glamorous, as well as intellectually stimulating.

We interviewed the senior editor of a publishing house one afternoon when she was negotiating for a manuscript. We sat in her spacious office with corner windows overlooking all of New York and listened to her bargain and cajole with the literary agent and make on-the-spot decisions with her staff. It's obviously a job where you have to think on your feet. When we asked for her advice on how to get into book publishing, she told us that the way to become an editor is to start as secretary to an editor. Since you'll find men as secretaries in publishing houses, as well as women, the competition for jobs is keen. Usually, an editor will give a secretary an early crack at reading manuscripts and writing critiques, so it's a great place to learn. From secretary, you can work your way up to editorial assistant or possibly copy editor (preparing a book for publication by correcting grammar and spelling, verifying facts, insuring style-consistency). From there, you're on your way to associate editor and editor.

It's a fascinating business, loaded with opportunities and, we might add, with women who've made it. A college major in English is ideal background and one editor mentioned that a summer job in a bookstore might be helpful.

Nobody goes into publishing for the money. Unless you write, or are agent for, a best-seller, the numbers really don't come close to some of the other glamour industries. Even so, it's a dream of a business for anyone in love with words and ideas.

For more information:

The American Book Publishers Council
One Park Avenue
New York, New York   10016

Magazine Publishing

The editorial staff of a magazine consists of the creative people who put the "book" together, choose or arrange for or write the articles, lay out the editorial content, and control what appears on the pages. The business staff handles circulation and advertising (known as "space" sales). Most major magazines have a large promotion department (as part of the business end of things) who work with advertisers to help them get the most mileage out of the ads they place in the book, as well as to assist the sales staff in effectively selling the magazine to prospective advertisers.

Editorial jobs vary, depending on the kind of magazine it is. This is the age of specialization, so a fashion editor leads a completely different life from that of a fiction or travel or features editor. Working on a news weekly is something else again. If you do have a particular interest—be it science, politics, women's rights, home furnishings, what have you—and want a glamorous career, a magazine is a terrific place to work. We've discussed the opportunities open to you on a fashion magazine, and the same holds true on any of the specialized books. A strong background in the subject matter of the particular magazine can put you a jump ahead of others competing for the same job. As in book publishing, magazine salaries are nothing to write home about, although the business jobs pay better (if you're in sales, anyway) than the editorial ones. The money improves as you make a name for yourself in the industry, but in general, magazines don't rival other glamour businesses in the remuneration department. Despite that, working for one can be wonderful. Since there's a new issue each month "to put to bed," there are new ideas and challenges to be met each month; that's fun. Magazines seem to have a warm familial quality about them, which makes day-to-day office life comfortable.

If you have sales abilities, don't overlook the possibility of a job selling advertising space for a magazine. Time was when magazines shied away from hiring women in this capacity because media *buyers* were mostly men. As with so many other areas of life, attitudes have changed in this regard, too. More and more media buyers are now women, for one thing; for another, magazines acknowledge today that women *can* take men to lunch as well as convince them of a magazine's efficacy. There's been enough time for the pioneer women, who broke down the "space sales" barriers, to prove themselves and, as a result, many magazines are scouting for women to fill these positions. It's an unusually glamorous *selling* job because it entails lots of lunches, cocktails, and socializing on the expense account. What's more, the money can turn out to be pretty respectable since part of the salary is often based on commission. Space salespeople usually specialize in product categories, such as liquor, cosmetics, or automobiles. The way in is through the business side of a magazine, starting in promotion or, perhaps, trying to sell the small space ads found in the back of the book.

If what you want is a career on the editorial staff, don't take a job on the business side of the magazine unless it's the only possible way in and you're promised a chance to cross over. The two sides usually operate without much interaction, so don't waste your time in an arena of no interest to you. Depending on your goals, a college major in English or commercial art will prepare you best. If you're planning a future in a "special interest" field, it obviously makes the most sense to major in a correlated subject.

Newspaper Publishing

The immediacy of newspaper work, the excitement of actually being a part of the *news* is pretty heady stuff. There's nothing more glamorous than being keyed into world events. No one has to tell you what's going on—you're there, on the inside, privy to all the facts. Newspaper offices traditionally are not plush or luxurious; they are crowded, hectic, utilitarian, and noisy. But what a place to work—with the pulse of the world at your fingertips! While there are many different kinds of jobs on newspapers, the heart of the action is reporting. Most people who dream of newspaper careers center their fantasies on becoming reporters. With good reason, too, because it's the reporter who's on the spot at the time things happen. It's the reporter's job to ferret out the story, see the event firsthand, and interview the newsmaker. It also falls to the reporter to research and verify the facts and prepare pertinent background material. The job takes drive and energy, but it's a thriller. "The pace is horrendous," a senior editor on the *New York Times* told us, "but it's the most exciting job there is."

If the idea of working on a newspaper enchants you and you have artistic talent, there are fine careers to be had as layout artist, cartoonist, or illustrator. Newspapers are actively looking for competent women now, though most women still find that jobs on the society or women's pages are easiest to come by. Most reporters get their first chance writing obituaries, then graduate to "small" stories. A newspaper veteran suggested that eager beginners on a paper should submit story ideas and copy to every department, and to make as many story suggestions as possible. It's the way to get a foot in the door; if you're good, you'll get a shot at bigger things.

Journalism school, or a college journalism major, can be helpful. Small-town newspaper experience or working for a magazine with a small staff (so you can get a crack at writing) can also give you an edge. You'll be a cut above other job applicants if you know the copy symbols in the back of the dictionary or have read the *New York Times* book on newspaper style.

For more information:

American Newspaper Publishing Association
750 Third Avenue
New York, New York   10017

Sigma Delta Chi
Professional Journalistic Society
35 East Wacker Driver
Chicago, Illinois   60601

Advertising

Advertising is a jet-propelled business with lots of opportunity for advancement and big money, but little job security. It's an industry that has always welcomed women, although in the past they were often relegated to working on "women's" accounts, such as beauty, fashion, food, and textiles. Today, women are making inroads into every corner of advertising, and it's not unusual to find a woman as president of her own agency. Mary Wells Lawrence, founder of Wells, Rich, Greene, is a striking example. Less than twenty years ago, "Bunny" Wells was a secretary at Doyle, Dane, Bernbach; today, she's one of the most famous, successful women in the world. That's one of the most glamorous things about advertising: if you have the talent, you can rise to the top quickly.

Good money and expense accounts are restricted to the top level in many industries, not so in advertising where even people on the way up are well-paid. One of the benefits of advertising is that you can move up the ladder swiftly; one of its pitfalls is that you can lose your footing just as easily. It's a service business with competitive agencies eager to please demanding clients. When you're hot, you're hot; when you miss once or twice, nobody knows your name. Advertising's reputation for giving ulcers is well-founded. If you thrive on competition, you'll love it. If you long for a comfortable place to hang your hat, it's not for you. There are rewards, though, to seeing your work produced. There's nothing quite like the gratification of hearing your words spoken on a TV commercial, seeing your graphics in print, finding the idea you fought for used as the cornerstone of a national campaign.

There are ad agencies and companies with advertising departments in every major city in the country (although New York and Chicago are conceded to be the best), so you won't necessarily have to move far from your hometown to break into the business. Your job is more secure if you work for a company because companies sometimes fire their advertising agencies, while the reverse is rarely true. There are fewer glamorous jobs available in a company, though, and those that do exist tend to be involved with the business—not the creative—end of things. Company jobs, therefore, are less desirable for someone starting out, hopeful of establishing a reputation in copy or art.

We'll concentrate on the structure of agencies, then, since the preponderance of glamour jobs are to be found there. The creative department consists of copywriters and art directors, who usually work in teams to produce the ads. These teams are supervised by creative directors; if the agency is a large one, the creative directors will have several teams working under them. On busy accounts, the art director may have an assistant and there may even be a junior copywriter. Production also falls within the domain of the creative department. In glamour terms, TV production is infinitely preferable to print production because producing a TV commercial is something akin to producing a mini-movie. The tried-and-true secretarial route is probably your best entrée into the creative department of an agency. If you're artistic, you might be able to land a job as an assistant art director or a spot in the "bullpen." (Just be sure you can get proof of promotion *out* of the bullpen.) As far as required background is concerned, a commercial art or writing major, or technical (film and tape) training will prove helpful.

There are several challenging business aspects in advertising. The marketing arm of an agency, called account management, oversees and coordinates all the work done at the agency for its clients. The account people act as agency liaison with the client and must be able to handle themselves well under pressure, know when to hold a client's hand, and when to stand up for the agency's point of view. Good writing skills are an asset here since the account group is directly involved in marketing the client's product (how to be more successful than the competition with the consumer) and often are required to prepare marketing plans. Two other "business" departments are media and research. If you're after a career in the business of advertising, you really should have a liberal arts background with an advanced degree in business administration, journalism, or marketing. You may well be able to skip the secretarial route if you have top-notch academic qualifications. In fact, agencies recruit employees directly from the ranks of graduating MBA candidates and journalism majors. If you don't have a graduate degree, you'll probably have to start behind a typewriter. Look for an agency that believes in promoting from its secretarial positions.

If you can maintain your equilibrium through the inevitable ups and downs, you'll find advertising an extremely rewarding field. In any service business, there's always the threat of losing the client and with that your job. If you're self-confident by nature and have an optimistic view of life, few industries can beat advertising for available opportunities and high-paying salaries.

For more information:

American Association of Advertising Agencies
200 Park Avenue
New York, New York   10017

American Advertising Federation
1225 Connecticut Avenue, N.W.
Washington, D.C.   20036

Women's Advertising Club of Chicago
400 West Madison Street
Chicago, Illinois   60606

PUBLIC RELATIONS

The business of public relations is to obtain free publicity, as opposed to paid advertising. A P.R.

firm provides the link between an organization and its public—be it the consumer, its employees, the financial community, or whatever segment of the population it wants to influence.

Public relations is less easy to categorize than some of the other glamour industries because there is little division between its creative and business functions. One person does the writing as well as establishing outside contacts. A P.R. person decides where to place an item she's written, or dreams up a promotional idea and implements it herself. This is unlike advertising, where separate departments handle the separate responsibilities. Obviously, a good promotional sense is required as well as keen administrative ability and excellent writing skills. It's a tall order, but for those of you with a vivid imagination and a head full of ideas, it may be the perfect field.

There is a vast difference in product P.R. and financial and public opinion P.R. Since most of the glamorous jobs seem to be involved in product or product-related public relations, we'll concentrate on the abilities and background necessary for that end of the business. Theatrical publicity is a very specialized category and particularly hard to break into; like so many businesses allied to the performing arts, it's unionized.

A P.R. person plants "news" releases in newspapers and magazines and arranges radio and TV coverage for "events" she has staged. She also gets her clients' names mentioned in industry news stories, writes company newsletters, house organs, and so on. A P.R. person is the public face of a company. She may travel around the country, acting as spokesperson for her client or speaking at industry functions. Public relations people entertain editors and other important contacts at the best restaurants; they travel first class and do their work in impressive offices—all in an effort to enhance their client's image.

The money is not as meager as in publishing, nor as munificent as in advertising. The fringe benefits are frequently fantastic; in fashion-related fields it's not at all unusual to have a clothing allowance for special events or to be able to charge hairdresser bills to the client. Meals, transportation, and necessary adjuncts to the job are not only the best, but at company expense. If the company is involved with celebrities, you're the contact. Certain P.R. firms deal almost exclusively with Hollywood, famous authors, and the like. They're on call day and night, arranging screenings, interviews, parties, and all sorts of excitement. The people in it swear the long hours don't matter; the work, they say, is fabulous and the people you meet sensational.

What's not so sensational is that you're always in a position where you have to please someone. If you work for a P.R. firm, you have to worry about the client. If you work directly for a company, you have to concern yourself with management. No matter which, you're always at the behest of the press, which can make you look good, or good and lousy. You're really at the whim of a variety of people, and that can be very difficult if your psyche isn't geared that way.

Besides the obvious need for excellent writing skills and administrative capabilities, a good eye for photography and illustration is often very helpful, because it's the P.R. person's job to arrange for whatever pictures accompany a story or do the layout of the newsletter. It's a job that calls for supreme tact and an ease in handling lots of different kinds of people. The ability to speak in public is not always required, but it's an asset. We might add that more and more P.R. women are finding their way onto local daytime TV talk shows. So if on-camera assignments interest you, a P.R. career might even lead to that goal.

A liberal arts degree with a major in English or journalism is the best background for a career in public relations. Newspaper experience is often helpful. If a specific field interests you (such as financial or political P.R.), it would be wise to have majored in a related subject in college. Graduate work in journalism or your area of special interest may well help you eliminate that first secretarial step. Public relations jobs can be found in just about any major city, but the best selections are in New York, Los Angeles, Chicago, and Washington.

For more information:

Career Information Service
Public Relations Society of America
845 Third Avenue
New York, New York   10022

BROADCASTING

Television is the communications vehicle of our age. As a nation, we're hooked. Americans spend more time in front of their TV sets than in any other recreational pursuit. It came as no surprise to us, then, to find that most of the young women we spoke to about careers were dreaming of jobs in television. In the past, the dream might have been to be in the movies or involved in some facet of fashion; today, it's TV all the way. For that reason, we'll concentrate on the opportunities TV has to offer, although much of our advice is relevant to radio as well.

Of the four main career areas in broadcasting—programming, administration, sales, and engineering—the first is, by far, the most glamorous. Women are beginning to make inroads into jobs selling time (as in its print counterpart, space sales, the doors are no longer barred), in administration, and even engineering. As a matter of fact, the day we visited the soap opera set, a young college woman was pushing one of the large TV cameras as part of an engineer training program; she seemed completely accepted and comfortable, to us. Nevertheless, these jobs are not going to be readily available. Programming strikes us as being more fertile ground.

Women have already proved to be successful in production, newswriting, casting, costume, and set decoration, as well as daytime and children's programming. Public affairs programming has also been a good area for women in television. Today, women are prominent on the air as anchorwomen and correspondents, unlike the recent past when there were token weathergirls or an occasional "women's story" reporter. If you watch the "crawl" (the credits at the end of a TV show), you'll find an increasing number of women's names as writers, producers, and directors.

Television jobs are in great demand, and women with backgrounds in communications, journalism, theater arts, or public speaking have a decided advantage. One production assistant said the best way to forge a TV career would be to go to a studio and take any secretarial position you can get. Once you're there, you can apply for any openings you hear about. Television is definitely an industry where secretaries get promoted. So, once again, the way in is as a secretary or, if you're lucky, as production assistant. Local stations are a great place to start. They're usually understaffed and you'll have a better chance to do different things and become more involved in the overall operation than on a major station. As we said before, working for a local station in a city that also has a network-owned-and-operated station can work to your benefit; you can gain experience on the smaller station and then switch. If you can get a job on one of the top networks, terrific; just be willing to work like a demon.

If someone were to ask what the ideal first job is, we'd say "show" secretary or production assistant. It's the perfect spot from which to learn, firsthand, how a show is put together and who does what. You can decide what direction you'd like your career to take after you're working at a station or on a show or for an independent production house.

Television is less structured than some of the other glamour industries in that job functions are more flexible. It's not at all unusual for a producer or a director to get an idea for a show and become a writer. Mary Kay Place was a writer's secretary on the *Maude* TV show. She learned how a half-hour TV script was constructed, and decided to try her hand at writing one. She showed her boss her *Maude* script, and he liked it well enough to produce it. What's more, that particular show won an Emmy. The Lear organization may have lost a secretary, but it gained a writer. To prove that you never know what can happen to you if you're in the right place at the right time, Mary Kay Place is now an actress, playing the part of Loretta Haggers on *Mary Hartman, Mary Hartman.* You guessed it, that show's also produced by Norman Lear.

Our producer friend, Karen (who got her break by bringing the director coffee), so impressed a superstar when she was production assistant on a network special that he hired her as associate producer when he got his own weekly show. The top brass felt Karen was really too junior for such responsibility, but the star insisted. He wrote her into his contract: no Karen, no show! If you're in a position to show what you can do, and perform your job splendidly, you can really go places in television.

For more information:

American Women in Radio and TV, Inc.
75 East 55th Street
New York, New York   10022

National Association of Broadcasters
1771 N. Street, N.W.
Washington, D.C.   20036

MOVIES

Ah, the lure of Hollywood. For consummate glamour, nothing comes close to the movies. No other industry quite captures the imagination the way the motion picture business does. All the pretty people, all the magnificent homes (in the most expensive real estate in the country), all the elements of the most lavish life-style—that's what we think of when we think movies. It's true, every superlative glamorous word. The problem is that we only see half the story. The movie business is a tough, hard-nosed one where you're only as good as your last picture, where people only remember the last deal you made. Careers rise and fall like the tides and women are supposed to be ornamental.

That isn't to say we're not bewitched by the movies. We are, but the industry may well be one of the staunchest strongholds of male chauvinism, and any woman thinking of a career in it had better be prepared for some rough going. (We're not addressing those of you who want to act; if you've been bitten by that bug, only God can help you.) Know it now, it is a disadvantage to be female. The attitudes tend to be Victorian, if not archaic. The pay is consistently lower than men's salaries and since certain areas are stereotyped as "good" for women, it's not easy to get into the others.

You're not dissuaded? Okay. First thing, head for Hollywood. Los Angeles is the movie capital of the world and that's where the action is. There are studio offices and sales and distribution offices in New York, as well as East Coast branches of some of the most important talent agencies, but your chances are better in California. In an industry where contacts are critical, the best place to make them is in L.A. Read the want ads in the trade papers and apply to studio personnel departments. Here again, women sometimes have the advantage over men because they can start as secretaries. Decide which area is of particular interest to you: set design, production, story analysis, and try to get a job in that department. Your secretarial skills had better be A-one, because the·competition is stiff. Once you're in, work like a whirlwind. Do more, be better, be worth promoting. Hollywood is a small town, and the word gets around very fast if someone's good (or bad). You may have to work for several people before you do get a break, but if you stick it out, the opportunity will present itself.

The "creative" and "business" functions of the industry are very closely intertwined, but most of the careers for women seem to fall into the more "creative" category. There are relatively few women in sales and distribution and only some in marketing (advertising, promotion and publicity). As for business affairs, a legal background seems to be the order of the day. Unfortunately, even in the "creative" end of the movie business, certain careers are in the pioneering stage, if not impossible, for women. There are almost no camerawomen and very few who are directors or producers. Film cutting and film editing are also especially difficult fields for women. On the other hand, casting and the "guild" areas (such as make-up or wardrobe) have always had a fair number of women in them. Studio story departments have historically been open to women.

Considering how hard it is for women to break into the motion picture industry, the following story—told to us by an associate producer—is a shocker. She placed an ad in the trade papers for a secretary. "A hundred women called about the job and half of them hung up when they learned they'd be working for a woman." Sometimes we work against our own best interests.

Film courses given at various schools are very good if you want a career *making* movies and need to learn special skills; they can also provide some contacts (which are always a help) and an overall awareness of the business. By and large, what matters more than a degree is doing the job well and having the ability to get along with people. If a job enables you to meet people, then it's not a dead end. There's an active grapevine, and when someone is looking for a good person to fill a vacant spot, the word goes out.

To make it in the movies, you have to be able to think big. There's a special mentality that comes from dealing in big numbers. The name of the game is to get the job done. If you have to talk to people in London, you fly there and talk to them. Life takes on a luxurious simplicity, because the cost doesn't matter. Creative energy is worth everything, as long you can deliver. Cities are built, bridges burned, screen rights purchased for dollars in the stratosphere. You can lose perspective; many do. It's called "going Hollywood." It's a fast track, but if you can stand the pace and keep your head, you'll love it.

"It's stimulating to the point of short-circuiting," one successful woman told us. That lady's day starts at 7:30, when she makes her calls to New York and London over breakfast coffee. She spoke to us at 8:30 at night, while she was grabbing dinner at her desk. "You cannot have a career like this half-heartedly. You have to fight for time for a private life." But like all the other women we interviewed, she wouldn't change jobs for anything. "You get to meet everybody sooner or later; you have access to any world you're interested in. There's total variety in a business like this and no way ever to be bored. The movies reach so many people and you feel as if you really have an impact on what people think."

We certainly understand why the motion picture business appeals to so many people. It goes beyond movie stars and fancy swimming pools. It's life on another scale and that translates into glamour. If moving to California is impossible for those of you irresistibly drawn by movie magnetism, try New York. As we said, some of the major companies have offices there, and you never know where a secretarial job will lead. One of the most successful and important women in the business started that way. Sue Mengers, a dynamic blonde with unlimited brain power, began her career as a secretary in the William Morris Agency. She's an extremely influential agent today, with such clients as Paul Newman and Barbra Streisand in her stable. We suggest you check our Glamour Job Yellow Pages for the New York offices of any company or agency that interests you.

As we said, getting into the more technical aspects of movie-making is not the easiest thing a woman can do, but if that's your dream, you'd better be properly qualified. One reentry woman told us she wangled a job in New York working on a documentary after she'd completed a course in film editing. As luck would have it, the film was the hit of that year's New York Film Festival, so other assignments followed. It happens.

What you have to do is be persistent; develop some skill, perhaps some special expertise in a tangential business—and then switch. It's been done before; people from TV, advertising, publicity and publishing have managed to cross over into the motion picture industry successfully. Maybe not in droves, but it's possible. We like to think you'll do it, too.

For more information:

American Film Institute
501 Doheny Road
Beverly Hills, California   90210

Academy of Motion Picture Arts & Sciences
8949 Wilshire Blvd.
Beverly Hills, California   90212

Women of the Motion Picture Industry
4600 Willis Ave. #107
Sherman Oaks, California   91403

❧ *The Glamour Job Yellow Pages*

The Glamour Job Yellow Pages contain our choices for the companies most likely to have glamour job possibilities in each industry. This is not a definitive list. We're sure your local library will have complete directories of advertising agencies, public relations firms, corporations (by industry), and so on. You can use them to augment our selections; just don't rely on them for current executive names. You'll also find we haven't included local TV stations and newspapers because we know that *you* know the ones in your particular area. We have listed the larger syndicates; if one is headquartered near you, contact it. Many of the advertising and public relations agencies listed have branch offices throughout the country. If one of them is near where you live, even if the office is a small one, it might be a good place to investigate. As we've said, prove yourself in your first job, and moving up (or to a larger office in a bigger city) should be no problem. You might even be able to transfer to a European branch office, if living in Europe is your fantasy.

The motion picture listing is not as extensive as the others because of the nature of the business. There are many, very small companies with only minimal job opportunities and we think it's pointless to enumerate them. We're only going to give you the companies in which we think you might have a chance. In addition to the major film studios, we have included the film production houses which often make films, or taped shows, for television. There is also a separate listing for the film industry's talent agencies, publicity agencies, and the largest advertising agency. Where there is a good-sized East Coast branch office, we've put that in, too.

Now, here's what to do if you want to contact any of these companies. If you have strong feelings about a specific area within a company, or know which division of it interests you, call the company and get the name of a director or vice-president in that area. Don't rely on directory listings for names! People change jobs and an inquiry addressed to the wrong person smacks of carelessness; it will look like you didn't do your homework. Many of you probably don't know exactly whom to approach; for first jobs, the personnel director is as good a person as any. Regardless of the person to whom you direct your inquiry, write a covering letter to send with your resumé. Say that you're eager to work in the such-and-such industry and think highly of company X's product, or advertising, or whatever, and would like to know about the possibility of an entry-level job. Add that you will call in a week to see if you can arrange an appointment for an interview. Remember to emphasize that you're looking for an *entry*-level job. At the interview, you should ask about the company's policy in regard to promoting from within, training programs, and the like. Don't forget to include such pertinent facts as your typing speed. If you already have specific work experience, or an area of special interest, state it in the letter even though your resumé will undoubtedly indicate your strengths. In *all* cases, send a letter with your resumé before you call for an interview.

GOOD LUCK!

FASHION

Women's Apparel Manufacturers

Aileen, Inc.
331 East 38th Street, New York, N.Y.
10016   212-679-7010

Alba-Waldensian, Inc.
P.O. Box 100, Valdese, N.C. 28690   704-874-2191

Bali Co., Inc.
666 Fifth Avenue, New York, N.Y.
10019   212-765-8900

Berkshire International Corp.
640 Fifth Avenue, New York, N.Y.
10019   212-581-8050

Bleeker Street
10101 Roosevelt Blvd., Philadelphia,
Pa. 19154   215-0R6-9200

Bobbie Brooks, Inc.
3830 Kelley Avenue, Cleveland, Ohio
44114   216-881-5300

Cole of California, Inc.
2615 Fruitland Avenue, Los Angeles,
Cal. 90058   213-587-3111

Country Miss, Inc.,
533 Seventh Avenue, New York, N.Y.
10018   212-564-7832

David Crystal, Inc.
  498 Seventh Avenue, New York, N.Y.
    10018   212-BR9-6560

Dalton Inc.
  Dalton Boulevard, Willoughby, Ohio
    44094   216-946-4000

Damon International
  16 East 34th Street, New York, N.Y.
    10016   212-683-2465

Danskin Inc.
  1114 Sixth Avenue, New York, N.Y.
    10036   212-869-9800

Devon Apparel, Inc.
  3300 Frankford Avenue, Philadelphia,
    Pa. 19134   215-RE9-2000

Donnkenny, Inc.
  1411 Broadway, New York, N.Y.
    10018   212-565-3770

Evan-Picone, Inc.
  1407 Broadway, New York, N.Y.
    10018   212-391-0770

Exquisite Form Industries
  14 Pelham Parkway, Pelham Manor,
    N.Y. 10803   914-PE8-2200

Formfit Rogers
  530 Fifth Avenue, New York, N.Y.
    10036   212-MU2-1333

Gay Gibson, Inc.
   8101 Lenexa Drive, P.O. Box 2014,
     Shawnee Mission, Kan. 66201   913-888-4600

H. W. Gossard Co.
   111N Canal, Chicago, Ill. 60606   312-AN3-0200

'Hanes Hosiery, Inc.
   P.O. Box 1413, Winston-Salem, N.C.
   27102   919-744-2011

Hanes Knitwear
   Winston-Salem, N.C. 27102   919-744-2011

International Playtex Corp.
   888 Seventh Avenue, New
     York, N.Y. 10019   212-957-3000

Jantzen Inc.
   P.O. Box 3001, Portland, Ore. 97208   503-234-9301

Jonathan Logan Inc.
   1411 Broadway, New York, N.Y.
   10018   212-695-4440

Kayser-Roth Corp.
   Catalina Div., 6040 Bandini Blvd.,
     L.A., Cal. 90040   213-726-1262

Kayser-Roth Intimate Apparel Co.
   640 Fifth Avenue, New York, N.Y.
   10019   212-PL7-9600

Kimberly Knitwear
   1441 Broadway, New York, N.Y.
   10018   212-221-7373

Lady Manhattan Co.
1407 Broadway, New York, N.Y.
10018   212-765-1250

L'Aiglon Apparel, Inc.
1400 Broadway, New York, N.Y.
10018   212-LW4-0800

Lanz Originals, Inc.
6150 Wilshire, Los Angeles,
Cal. 90048   213-WE7-1400

L'Eggs Products Inc.
P.O. Box 2495, Winston-Salem, N.C.
27102   919-744-2768

Leslie Fay Inc.
1400 Broadway, New York, N.Y.
10018   212-221-4000

Lily of France, Inc.
90 Park Avenue, New York, N.Y.
10016   212-392-2200

Loveable Co.
200 Madison Avenue, New York, N.Y.
10016   212-686-7788

Maidenform, Inc.
90 Park Avenue, New York, N.Y.
10016   212-687-4900

Munsingwear Inc.
Vassarette Div., 718 Glenwood
Avenue, Minneapolis, Minn. 55405   612-340-4700

Olga Co.
7900 Haskell Avenue, Van Nuys, Cal.
91406 · 213-782-7568

Puritan Fashions Corp.
1400 Broadway, New York, N.Y.
10018 212-OX5-7900

Round-the-Clock Hosiery
350 Fifth Avenue, New York, N.Y.
10001 212-BR9-8210

Abe Schrader Corp.
530 Seventh Avenue, New
York, N.Y. 10018 212-LO4-9194

Serbin Fashions Inc.
3480 N.W. 41st Street, Miami, Fla.
33142 305-635-0607

J. P. Stevens Hosiery Div.
1185 Avenue of the Americas, New
York, N.Y. 10036 212-575-3400

Van Raalte Co., Inc.
417 Fifth Avenue, New York, N.Y.
10016 212-MU9-4200

Vanity Fair Mills, Inc.
1047 N. Park Road, Wyomissing,
Pa. 19610 215-376-7201

Warnaco Inc.
Warner's Div., 325 Lafayette, Bridge-
port, Conn. 06602 203-333-1151

White Stag Mfg. Co.
   5100 S.E. Harney Drive, Portland,
      Ore. 97206   503-777-1711

Jack Winter
   8100 N. Teutonia Avenue, Milwaukee,
      Wis. 53223   414-354-4100

Accessories & Shoes

G. H. Bass & Co.
   Wilton, Me. 04294   207-645-2556

Brown Group Inc.
   8400 Maryland Avenue, St. Louis,
      Mo. 63105   314-997-7500

Buxton Inc.
   265 Main, Agawam, Mass. 01001   413-786-7000

Cobblers, Inc.
   8780 National Blvd., Culver City, Cal.
      90230   213-870-4881

Coro Inc.
   47 West 34th Street, New York, N.Y.
      10001   212-947-1329

Desco Shoe Corp.
   16 East 34th Street, New York, N.Y.
      10016   212-MU3-2600

Napier Co.
   530 Fifth Avenue, New York, N.Y.
      10036   212-YU6-6633

Olga Tritt, Inc.
  424 Park Avenue, New York, N.Y.
    10022   212-PL5-8379

Sarah Coventry, Inc.
  Newark, N.Y. 14593   315-331-6900

Stride Rite Corp.
  960 Harrison Avenue, Boston, Mass.
    02118   617-440-9300

Swank, Inc.
  90 Park Avenue, New York, N.Y.
    10016   212-TN7-2600

Town & Country Shoes, Inc.
  7745 Carondelet, Clayton, Mo. 63105   314-862-1500

United States Shoe Corp.
  1658 Herald Avenue, Cincinnati, Ohio
    45212   513-841-4111

Wohl Shoe Co.
  8350 Maryland Avenue, Clayton, Mo.
    63105   314-863-9000

Wolverine Worldwide, Inc.
  9341 Courtland Drive, Rockford,
    Mich. 49351   616-866-1561

Textile & Home Sewing

Beaunit Corp.
  261 Madison Avenue, New York, N.Y.
    10016   212-972-3200

Blue Ridge-Winkler Textiles
119 West 40th Street, New York, N.Y.
10018   212-947-8800

Burlington Industries, Inc.
1345 Avenue of the Americas, New
York, N.Y. 10019   212-333-5000

Butterick Fashion Marketing Co.
161 Avenue of the Americas, New
York, N.Y. 10013   212-620-2500

Celanese Fibers Co.
1211 Avenue of the Americas, New
York, N.Y. 10019   212-764-7640

Cohn-Hall-Marx Co.
1407 Broadway, New York, N.Y. 10018   212-564-6000

Collins & Aikman Corp.
210 Madison Avenue, New York, N.Y.
10016   212-MU9-3900

Columbia-Minerva Corp.
295 Fifth Avenue, New York, N.Y.
10016   212-MU5-2907

Cone Mills Marketing Co.
1440 Broadway, New York, N.Y.
10018   212-LO5-4600

Courtaulds North America, Inc.
104 West 40th Street, New York, N.Y.
10018   212-LW4-1600

Crompton Co., Inc.
  1071 Avenue of the Americas, New
    York, N.Y. 10018   212-564-2900

Dan River Inc.
  McAlister Plaza, Greenville, S.C.
    29606   803-242-5950

Deering Milliken, Inc.
  1045 Avenue of the Americas, New
    York, N.Y. 10018   212-695-1200

Indian Head Inc.
  1211 Avenue of the Americas, New
    York, N.Y. 10036   212-764-3100

M. Lowenstein & Sons, Inc.
  1430 Broadway, New York, N.Y.
    10018   212-OX5-5000

McCall Pattern Co.
  230 Park Avenue, New York, N.Y.
    10016   212-983-3200

Riegel Textile Corp.
  260 Madison Ave., New York, N.Y.
    10016   212-883-5600

Simplicity Pattern Co., Inc.
  200 Madison Avenue, New York, N.Y.
    10016   212-OR9-3700

West Point Pepperell Alamac Knitting
Div.
  1412 Broadway, New York, N.Y.
    10018   212-354-9150

RETAILING

Abraham & Straus
420 Fulton Street, Brooklyn, N.Y.
11201   212-TR9-5720

Allied Stores Corp.
1114 Avenue of the Americas, New
York, N.Y. 10036   212-764-2000

B. Altman
Fifth Avenue at 34th Street, New
York, N.Y. 10016   212-OR9-7800

Associated Dry Goods Corp.
417 Fifth Avenue, New York, N.Y.
10016   212-OR9-8700

L. S. Ayres & Co.
1 W. Washington Street, Indianapolis,
Ind. 46204   317-262-4411

Battelstein's
812 Main, Houston, Tex. 77002   713-228-8822

Henri Bendel Inc.
10 West 57th Street, New York, N.Y.
10019   212-CI7-1100

Bergdorf Goodman
2 West 58th Street, New York, N.Y.
10019   212-PL3-7300

Bloomingdale's
Lexington Avenue and 59th Street,
New York, N.Y. 10022   212-752-1212

Bonwit Teller
721 Fifth Avenue, New York, N.Y.
10022   212-EL5-6800

Boston Store
331 W. Wisconsin Avenue, Milwaukee,
Wis. 53203   414-347-4141

Broadway Dept. Stores Inc.
3880 N. Mission Road, Los Angeles,
Cal. 90031   213-223-2266

Bullock's
659 South Broadway, Los Angeles,
Cal. 90014   213-486-5151

Burdine's
22 E. Flagler, Miami, Fla. 33131   305-835-5151

Carson Pirie Scott & Co.
1 S. State, Chicago, Ill. 60603   312-744-2000

Carter Hawley Hale Stores, Inc.
600 S. Spring Street, Los Angeles, Cal.
90014   213-620-0150

Dayton's
700 on the Mall, Minneapolis, Minn.
55402   612-375-2200

Famous Barr Co.
6th and Olive Street, St. Louis, Mo.
63101   314-GA1-5900

The Glamour Job Yellow Pages ⌦

Federated Dept. Stores, Inc.
  222 West Seventh Street, Cincinnati,
    Ohio 45202   513-852-3000

Marshall Field & Co.
  111 N. State, Chicago, Ill. 60690   312-ST1-1000

William Filene's Sons Co.
  426 Washington, Boston, Mass. 02101 617-426-3800

Foley's
  1110 Main, Houston, Tex. 77001   713-228-3311

Franklin Simon
  560 Washington, New York, N.Y.
    10014   212-675-1000

Frost Bros.
  217 E. Houston St., San Antonio, Tex.
    78205   512-CA6-7131

Garfinckel's
  F and 14th Streets, N.W., Washington,
    D.C. 20004   202-NA8-7730

Gimbels
  Broadway at 33rd Street, New York,
    N.Y. 10001   212-PE6-5100

Goldblatt Bros.
  333 S. State Street, Chicago, Ill. 60604 312-786-2000

Goldwaters
  3100 N. Central Avenue, Phoenix,
    Ariz. 80512   602-248-2626

Hecht Co.
  F at 7th Street, N.W., Washington,
    D.C. 20004   202-628-5100

Higbee Co.
  Public Square, Cleveland, Ohio 44113   216-579-2580

D. H. Holmes Co. Ltd.
  819 Canal, New Orleans, La. 70112   504-524-6611

J. L. Hudson Co.
  1206 Woodward, Detroit, Mich.
    48226   313-223-5100

Hutzler's
  212 No. Howard, Baltimore, Md.
    21201   301-727-1234

Jacobson Stores
  1200 N. West, Jackson, Mich. 49202   517-787-3600

Jordan Marsh Co.
  450 Washington, Boston, Mass.
    02107   617-HA6-9000

Joske's of Texas
  Alamo Plaza, San Antonio, Tex.
    78206   512-CA7-4343

Kaufmann's
  400 Fifth Avenue, Pittsburgh, Pa.
    15219   412-281-1000

Lord & Taylor
  424 Fifth Avenue, New York, N.Y.
    10018   212-WI7-3300

R. H. Macy & Co. Inc.
151 West 34th Street, New York, N.Y.
10001   212-OX5-4400

I. Magnin & Co.
Union Square, San Francisco, Cal.
94108   415-362-2100

Joseph Magnin Co., Inc.
59 Harrison Street, San Francisco,
Cal. 94105   415-433-4224

May D. & F.
16th at Tremont Place, Denver, Col.
80202   303-292-6000

May Dept. Stores Co.
6th and Olive Streets, St. Louis, Mo.
63101   314-436-3300

Miller & Rhoads
Richmond, Va. 23261   804-M18-3111

Montgomery Ward & Co.
535 W. Chicago Avenue, Chicago, Ill.
60607   312-467-2000

Neiman-Marcus Co.
Main & Ervay, Dallas, Tex. 75201   214-RI1-6911

Ohrbachs
5 West 34th Street, New York, N.Y.
10001   212-564-3100

J. C. Penney Co., Inc.
1301 Avenue of the Americas, New
York, N.Y. 10019   212-957-4321

H & S Pogue Co.
4th & Race, Cincinnati, Ohio 45202   513-381-4700

Rich's Inc.
45 Broad S.W., Atlanta, Ga. 30302   404-586-4636

J. W. Robinson Co.
7th & Grand, Los Angeles, Cal.
90017   213-MA8-0333

Sakowitz
Main & Dallas Avenue, Houston, Tex.
77002   713-224-1111

Saks Fifth Avenue
611 Fifth Avenue, New York, N.Y.
10022   212-PL3-4000

Sanger-Harris Stores
Pacific & Akard, Dallas, Tex. 75222   214-651-2345

Sear's Roebuck & Co.
Sears Tower, Chicago, Ill. 60684   312-875-2500

Strawbridge & Clothier
8th and Market Streets, Philadelphia,
Pa. 19105   215-WA2-7100

Thalhimer Bros. Inc.
615 E. Broad, Richmond, Va. 23219   804-643-4211

Titche-Goettinger
1901 Main St., Dallas, Tex. 75201   214-RI8-4811

John Wanamaker
13th & Market, Philadelphia, Pa.
19101   215-422-2000

Woodward & Lothrop
  10th, 11th, F & G, N.W., Washington,
    D.C. 20013   202-347-5300

BEAUTY: COSMETICS, HAIR GOODS, PERFUMES, TOILETRIES

Alberto-Culver Co.
  2525 Armitage Avenue, Melrose Park,
    Ill. 60160   212-531-2000

Almay, Inc.
  562 Fifth Avenue, New York, N.Y.
    10036   212-246-6900

Avon Products, Inc.
  9 West 57th Street, New York, N.Y.
    10019   212-593-4017

Beecham Inc.
  65 Industrial South, Clifton, N.J.
    07012   201-778-9000

Bonne-Bell Inc.,
  Georgetown Row, 18519 Detroit
    Avenue, Lakewood, Ohio 44107   216-221-0800

John H. Breck Inc.
  Berdan Avenue, Wayne, N.J. 07470   201-831-1234

Bristol-Meyers Company
  345 Park Avenue, New York, N.Y.
    10022   212-644-2100

Campana Corp.
  Batavia, Ill. 60510   312-TR9-3400

Carter-Wallace, Inc.
  767 Fifth Avenue, New York, N.Y.
  10022   212-758-4500

Chanel Inc.
  9 West 57th Street, New York, N.Y.
  10019   212-MU8-5055

Cheesebrough-Ponds, Inc.
  33 Benedict Place, Greenwich, Conn.
  06830   203-661-2000

Clairol Inc.
  345 Park Avenue, New York, N.Y.
  10022   212-644-3100

Colgate-Palmolive Co.
  300 Park Avenue, New York, N.Y.
  10022   212-PL1-1200

Cosmair, Inc.
  530 Fifth Avenue, New York, N.Y.
  10036   212-697-5115

Cosmetically Yours, Inc.
  100 River Street, Hastings-on-Hudson,
  N.Y. 10706   914-478-1000

Coty Div. of Pfizer, Inc.
  235 East 42nd Street, New York, N.Y.
  10017   212-573-3500

Dana Perfumes Corp.
  625 Madison Avenue, New York, N.Y.
  10022   212-751-3700

Dell Laboratories, Inc.
565 Broad Hollow Road, Farmingdale,
L.I., N.Y. 11735   516-293-7070

Dorothy Gray–Tussy Ltd.
225 Summit Avenue, Montvale, N.J.
07645   201-391-8500

Elizabeth Arden
1345 Avenue of the Americas, New
York, N.Y. 10019   212-399-2000

Estée Lauder
767 Fifth Avenue, New York, N.Y.
10022   212-826-3600

Evyan Perfumes, Inc.
350 E. 35th Street, New York, N.Y.
10016   212-LE2-3800

Faberge Inc.
1345 Avenue of the Americas, New
York, N.Y. 10019   212-581-3500

Frances Denney
630 Fifth Avenue, New York, N.Y.
10020   212-977-8400

Germaine Monteil Cosmetics Corp.
40 West 57th Street, New York, N.Y.
10019   212-582-3010

Gillette Co.
Prudential Tower Bldg., Boston, Mass.
02199   617-421-7000

Glemby Co., Inc.
120 East 16th Street, New York, N.Y.
10003   212-GR7-4700

Guerlain Inc.
444 Madison Avenue, New York, N.Y.
10022   212-PL1-1870

Helena Rubinstein Inc.
Northern Blvd. at East Hills, Green-
vale, N.Y. 11548   516-484-5400

Helen Curtis Industries
4401 W. North Avenue, Chicago, Ill.
60639   312-292-2121

Houbigant Inc.
1135 Pleasant View Terrace West,
Ridgefield, N.J. 07657   201-941-3400

Jacqueline Cochran Inc.
630 Fifth Avenue, New York, N.Y.
10020   212-489-2430

Andrew Jergens Co.
2535 Spring Grove, Cincinnati, Ohio
45214   513-421-1400

Jovan, Inc.
875 N. Michigan Avenue, Chicago,
Ill. 60611   312-787-2929

Lanvin–Charles of the Ritz Inc.
40 West 57th Street, New York, N.Y.
10019   212-489-4500

The Glamour Job Yellow Pages ❧

Lehn & Fink Products Co.
225 Summit Avenue, Montvale, N.J.
07645   201-391-8500

Max Factor & Co.
1655 No. McCadden Place, Hollywood, Cal. 90028   213-462-6131

Maybelline Co.
3030 Jackson Avenue, Memphis,
Tenn. 38101   901-320-2011

Mem Co. Inc.
Northvale, N.J. 07647   201-767-0100

Mennen Co.
Hanover Avenue, Morristown, N.J.
07960   201-538-7100

Noxell Corp.
11050 York Road, Baltimore, Md.
21203   301-666-2662

Pantene Co.
340 Kingsland Avenue, Nutley, N.J.
07110   201-235-4133

Pfizer Inc. Leeming/Paquin Div.
235 E. 42nd Street, New York, N.Y.
10017   212-LR3-3131

Prince Matchabelli
33 Benedict Place, Greenwich, Conn.
06830   203-661-2000

Redken Labs., Inc.
14721 California Avenue, Van Nuys,
Cal. 91401   213-781-4484

203 ❧

Revlon, Inc.
767 Fifth Avenue, New York, N.Y.
10022   212-758-5000

Sea & Ski Corp.
1500 Spring Garden Street, Phila-
delphia, Pa. 19101   215-LO4-2400

Shulton, Inc.
697 Rte. 46, Clifton, N.J. 07015   201-546-7000

Texas Pharmacal Co.
P.O. Box 1659, San Antonio, Tex.
78296   512-223-3281

PUBLISHING: BOOK, MAGAZINE, AND NEWSPAPER

American Girl Magazine
830 Third Avenue, New York, N.Y.
10022   212-PL1-6900

American Heritage Publishing Co., Inc.
1221 Avenue of the Americas, New
York, N.Y. 10020   212-997-1221

American Home Magazine
641 Lexington Avenue, New York,
N.Y. 10022   212-644-0300

Bantam Books Inc.
666 Fifth Avenue, New York, N.Y.
10019   212-765-6500

The Glamour Job Yellow Pages ✄

Basic Books
10 East 53rd Street, New York, N.Y.
10022   212-593-7057

Billboard Publications, Inc.
1 Astor Place, New York, N.Y. 10036   212-764-7300

Book-of-the-Month Club, Inc.
280 Park Avenue, New York, N.Y.
10017   212-867-4300

Boston Daily and Sunday Globe
135 Morrissey Blvd., Boston, Mass.
02107   617-929-2000

Buffalo Courier-Express
787 Main, Buffalo, New York 14240   716-847-5590

Butterick Fashion Marketing Co.
161 Sixth Avenue, New York, N.Y.
10013   212-620-2500

Cedar Rapids Gazette
500 Third Avenue S.E., Cedar Rapids,
Iowa 52406   319-398-8211

Chicago Daily News
401 N. Wabash, Chicago, Ill. 60611   312-321-2000

Chicago Sun Times
401 N. Wabash, Chicago, Ill. 60611   312-321-3000

Chicago Tribune
435 N. Michigan Avenue, Chicago, Ill.
60611   312-222-3232

Cincinnati Enquirer
617 Vine, Cincinnati, Ohio 45201   513-721-2700

Cincinnati Post
  8th and Broadway, Cincinnati, Ohio
    45202   513-721-1111

Cleveland Press
  East 9th and Lakeside Ave., Cleve-
    land, Ohio 44114   216-623-1111

Columbus Dispatch and Columbus
  Citizen Journal
    34 S. 3rd, Columbus, Ohio 43216   614-461-5000

Condé Nast Publications Inc.
  350 Madison Avenue, New York, N.Y.
    10017   212-692-5500

Courier Journal and Louisville Times
  525 W. Broadway, Louisville, Ky.
    40202   502-582-4011

Coward, McCann & Geoghegan, Inc.
  200 Madison Avenue, New York, N.Y.
    10016   212-886-5500

Thos. Y. Crowell Co., Inc.
  666 Fifth Avenue, New York, N.Y.
    10019   212-489-2200

Crown Publishers
  1 Park Avenue, New York,
    N.Y. 10016   212-532-9200

Cue Publishing Co., Inc.
  20 West 43rd Street, New York, N.Y.
    10036   212-LO3-7170

Curtis Publishing Co.
1100 Waterway Blvd. Indianapolis,
   Ind. 46202   317-634-1100

Daily Oklahoman and Oklahoma City
   Times
   P.O. Box 25125, Oklahoma City,
      Okla. 73125   405-232-3311

Dallas Morning News
   Dallas, Tex. 75222   214-745-8222

Dell Publications Co. Inc.
1 Dag Hammarskjold Plaza, New
   York, N.Y. 10017   212-832-7300

Denver Post
   650 15th, Denver, Colo. 80202   303-297-1010

Des Moines Register and Tribune
   715 Locust, Des Moines, Iowa 50304   515-284-8000

Detroit Free Press
321 West Lafayette Avenue, Detroit,
   Mich. 48231   313-222-6400

Detroit News
615 Lafayette Blvd., Detroit, Mich.
   48231   313-222-2000

Dial Press
1 Dag Hammarskjold Plaza, New
   York, N.Y. 10017   212-832-7300

Dodd, Mead & Co.
79 Madison Avenue, New York, N.Y.
   10016   212-MU5-6464

Doubleday & Co., Inc.
  245 Park Avenue, New York, N.Y.
  10017   212-935-4561

E. P. Dutton & Co., Inc.
  201 Park Avenue South, New York,
  N.Y. 10003   212-OR4-5900

El Paso Times
  401 Mills Street, El Paso, Texas 79901   915-532-1661

Esquire Inc.
  488 Madison Avenue, New York, N.Y.
  10022   212-759-3232

Eugene Register-Guard
  975 High Street, Eugene, Ore. 97401   503-485-1234

Family Circle Inc.
  488 Madison Avenue, New York, N.Y.
  10022   212-593-8000

Farrar Straus & Giroux Inc.
  19 Union Square W., New York, N.Y.
  10003   212-741-6900

Fawcett Publications, Inc.
  1515 Broadway, New York, N.Y.
  10036   212-869-3000

Gentlemen's Quarterly Magazine
  488 Madison Avenue, New York, N.Y.
  10022   212-644-5720

Grosset & Dunlap, Inc.
  51 Madison Avenue, New York, N.Y.
  10010   212-MU9-9200

Harcourt Brace Jovanovich, Inc.
757 Third Avenue, New York, N.Y.
10017   212-572-5000

Harper & Row Publishers, Inc.
10 East 53rd Street, New York, N.Y.
10022   212-593-7000

Hawaii Newspaper Agency, Inc.
605 Kapiolani Blvd., Honolulu, Hi.
96813   808-536-7222

Hearst Corp.
57th St. and Eighth Avenue, New York,
N.Y. 10019   212-262-5700

Houghton Mifflin Co.
2 Park, Boston, Mass. 02107   617-725-5000

Houston Chronicle
801 Texas, Houston, Tex. 77002   713-220-7171

Houston Post
4747 Southwest Freeway, Houston,
Tex. 77001   713-621-7000

Indianapolis Star and News
307 N. Pennsylvania, Indianapolis,
Ind. 46206   317-633-1240

Johnson Publishing Co.
820 S. Michigan Avenue, Chicago,
Ill. 60605   312-786-7600

Kansas City Star
Kansas City, Mo. 64108   816-421-1200

Knight-Ridder Newspapers Inc.
1 Herald Plaza, Miami, Fla. 33101   305-350-2082

Alfred A. Knopf Inc.
201 East 50th Street, New York, N.Y.
10022   212-PL1-2600

Knoxville News Sentinel Co.
208 West Church, Knoxville, Tenn.
37901   615-523-3131

Ladies Home Journal
641 Lexington Avenue, New York,
N.Y. 10022   212-935-4100

Lane Publishing Co.
Middlefield Road, Menlo Park, Cal.
94025   415-321-3600

J. B. Lippincott Co.
E. Washington Square, Philadelphia,
Pa. 19105   215-WA5-4100

Literary Guild of America Inc.
245 Park Avenue, New York, N.Y.
10017   212-953-4561

Little, Brown & Co.
34 Beacon, Boston, Mass. 02106   617-227-0730

Los Angeles Herald-Examiner
Box 2416 Terminal Annex, Los
Angeles, Cal. 90051   213-RI8,1212

Macmillan, Inc.
866 Third Avenue, New York, N.Y.
10022   212-935-2000

Madison Newspapers Inc.
115 S. Carroll St., P.O. Box 989
Madison, Wis. 53701   608-256-5511

McCall Pattern Co.
McCall Publishing Co.
230 Park Avenue, New York, N.Y.
10017   212-983-3200

McGraw-Hill
1221 Avenue of the Americas, New
York, N.Y. 10020   212-997-1221

David McKay Inc.
750 Third Avenue, New York, N.Y.
10017   212-MO1-1700

Memphis Publishing Co.
495 Union Avenue, Memphis, Tenn.
38101   901-526-8811

Meredith Corp.
1716 Locust Street, Des Moines,
Iowa 50336   515-284-9011

Miami Herald
Miami, Fla. 33101   305-350-2111

Milwaukee Journal
Milwaukee Sentinel
Journal Square, Milwaukee, Wis.
53201   414-224-2000

Minneapolis Star and Minneapolis
Tribune
425 Portland Avenue, Minneapolis,
Minn. 55415   612-372-4141

Wm. Morrow & Co.
105 Madison Avenue, New York, N.Y.
10016   212-889-3050

National Observer
22 Courtland Street, New York, N.Y.
10007   212-285-5000

New American Library
1301 Avenue of the Americas, New
York, N.Y. 10019   212-956-3800

New Republic
1244 19th, N.W., Washington, D.C.
20036   202-331-7494

New York Daily News
220 East 42nd Street, New York, N.Y.
10017   212-682-1234

New York Post
210 South Street, New York, N.Y.
10002   212-349-5000

New York Times
229 West 43rd Street, New York, N.Y.
10036   212-556-1234

New Yorker Magazine
25 West 43rd Street, New York, N.Y.
10036   212-OX5-1515

Newsweek Magazine
444 Madison Avenue, New York,
N.Y. 10022   212-350-2000

Oklahoma Publishing Co.
  P.O. Box 25125, Oklahoma City, Okla.
   73125   405-232-3311

1001 Communications Co.
  149 Fifth Avenue, New York, N.Y.
   10010   212-677-0870

Oregon Journal
Oregonian
  1320 S.W. Broadway, Portland, Ore.
   97201   503-221-8282

Pantheon Books, Div. of Random
   House, Inc.
  201 E. 50th Street, New York, N.Y.
   10016   212-PL1-2600

Parade Publications, Inc.
  733 Third Ave., New York, N.Y.
   10017   212-953-7500

Parent's Magazine Enterprises, Inc.
  52 Vanderbilt Ave., New York, N.Y.
   10017   212-MU5-4400

Penguin Books, Inc.
  72 Fifth Ave., New York, N.Y. 10011   212-924-8801

Philadelphia Daily News
  400 N. Broad Street, Philadelphia, Pa.
   19101   215-LO3-5200

Pittsburgh Post Gazette
  50 Boulevard of Allies, Pittsburgh, Pa.
   15222   412-263-1100

Pittsburgh Press
  Box 566, Pittsburgh, Pa. 15230   412-263-1100

Plain Dealer
  E. 18th & Superior, Cleveland, Ohio
  44114   216-523-4500

Popular Library Publishers
  600 Third Ave., New York, N.Y. 10016   212-661-4200

Praeger Publishers
  200 Park Ave., New York, N.Y. 10017   212-949-8700

G. P. Putnam's Sons
  200 Madison Ave., New York,
  N.Y. 10016   212-883-5500

Quadrangle/The New York Times Book Co.
  Three Park Ave., New York, N.Y.
  10016   212-725-2050

Random House, Inc.
  201 E. 50th Street, New York, N.Y.
  10016   212-883-5500

Reader's Digest Association, Inc.
  Pleasantville, N.Y. 10570   914-769-7000

Redbook Publishing Co.
  230 Park Avenue, New York, N.Y.
  10017   212-983-3200

Richmond Newspapers Inc.
  333 E. Grace Street, Richmond, Va.
  23219   804-649-6000

St. Louis Globe-Democrat
12th Blvd. at Delmar, St. Louis, Mo.
   63101   314-342-1212

St. Louis Post-Dispatch
900 North 12th Blvd., St. Louis, Mo.
   63101   314-621-1111

San Jose Mercury and News
750 Ridder Park Drive, San Jose,
   Cal. 95190   408-289-5000

Chas. Scribner's Sons
597 Fifth Avenue, New York, N.Y.
   10017   212-486-2700

Seattle Post-Intelligencer
6th & Wall, Seattle, Wash. 98121   206-MA2-2000

Seattle Times
Fairview No. & John, P.O. Box 70,
   Seattle, Wash. 98111   206-622-0300

Seventeen Magazine
320 Park Avenue, New York, N.Y.
   10022   212-751-8100

Simon & Schuster Inc.
630 Fifth Avenue, New York, N.Y.
   10020   212-CI5-6400

Stauffer Publications Inc.
6th & Jefferson, Topeka, Kan. 66607   913-357-4421

Sunday
260 Madison Avenue, New York, N.Y.
   10016   212-689-8200

TV Guide Magazine
    Radnor, Pa. 19088   215-MU8-7400

Time Inc.
    Time & Life Building, Rockefeller
    Center, New York, N.Y. 10020   212-JU6-1212

Times Mirror Co.
    Times Mirror Square, Los Angeles,
    Cal. 90053   213-486-3700

Times-Picayune Publishing Corp.
    3800 Howard Avenue, New Orleans,
    La. 70140   504-586-3785

Toledo Blade Co.
    541 Superior Street, Toledo, Ohio
    43660   419-259-6000

Tower Press Inc.
    Folly Mill Road, Seabrook, N.H.
    03874   603-474-3587

Tribune Publishing Co.
    401 13th, Oakland, Cal. 94612   415-645-2000

Union-Tribune Publishing Co.
    940 3rd Avenue, San Diego, Cal.
    92101   714-234-7111

U.S. News & World Report
    2300 N Street, N.W., Washington,
    D.C. 20037   202-FE3-7400

Viking Press Inc.
    625 Madison Avenue, New York, N.Y.
    10022   212-PL5-4330

Village Voice Inc.
  80 University Place, New York, N.Y.
  10003   212-741-0030

Wall Street Journal
  22 Courtland Street, New York, N.Y.
  10007   212-285-5000

Warner Paperback Library
  75 Rockefeller Plaza, New York, N.Y.
  10020   212-484-8000

Washington Star Communications Inc.
  225 Virginia Avenue, S.E., Washington, D.C. 20003   202-484-5000

Woman's Day
  1515 Broadway, New York, N.Y.
  10036   212-869-3000

Womensports Publishing Co.
  1660 S. Amphlett Blvd., San Mateo,
  Cal. 94402   415-574-4622

Ziff-Davis Publishing Co.
  1 Park Avenue, New York, N.Y. 10016   212-725-3500

ADVERTISING AGENCIES

Carl Ally, Inc.
  437 Madison Avenue, New York,
  N.Y. 10022   212-MU8-5300
  10889 Wilshire Blvd., Los Angeles,
  Cal. 90024   213-477-6511

N. W. Ayer
  1345 Avenue of the Americas, New
    York, N.Y. 10019   212-974-7400
  W. Washington Square, Philadelphia,
    Pa. 19106   215-829-4000
  One Illinois Center, 111 E. Wacker
    Drive, Chicago, Ill. 60601   312-645-8800

Barickman Advertising Inc.
  427 West 12th, Kansas City, Mo.
    64105   816-421-1000
  711 Fifth Avenue, New York, N.Y.
    10022   212-593-1620
  Greenwood Plaza, P.O. Box 9569,
    Denver, Col. 80209   303-770-4500

Ted Bates & Co., Inc.
  1515 Broadway, New York, N.Y.
    10036   212-869-3131

BBD&O
(Batten, Barten, Durstine & Osborn,
  Inc.)
  383 Madison Avenue, New York, N.Y.
    10017   212-355-5800
  2300 Prudential Center, Boston, Mass.
    02199   617-267-7800
  P.O. Box 3128 Gen. Post Station,
    Detroit, Mich. 48232   313-879-2000
  5670 Wilshire Blvd., Los Angeles, Cal.
    90036   213-938-3188
  1640 Northwestern Bank Bldg.,
    Minneapolis, Minn. 55402   612-338-8401
  650 California Street, San Francisco,
    Cal. 94108   415-397-1122

Benton & Bowles, Inc.
909 Third Avenue, New York, N.Y.
    10022   212-758-6200
1800 N. Highland Avenue,
    Hollywood, Cal. 90028   213-464-9151
233 N. Michigan Avenue, Chicago,
    Ill. 60601   312-861-0300

Bozell & Jacobs Inc.
One Dag Hammarskjold Plaza, New
    York, N.Y. 10017   212-644-7200
500 Bozell & Jacobs Plaza, 10250
    Regency Circle, Omaha, Neb.
    68114   402-397-8660
222 S. Riverside Plaza, Chicago, Ill.
    60606   312-648-1177
Two Northside 75, Atlanta, Ga.
    30318   404-352-1472
100 W. Washington, Phoenix, Ariz.
    85003   602-254-6451
Butler Square, 100 N. Sixth St.,
    Minneapolis, Minn. 55403   612-339-0071

Leo Burnett Co.
Prudential Plaza, Chicago, Ill. 60601   312-236-5959
6255 Sunset Blvd., Hollywood, Cal.
    90028   213-HO4-7373
767 Fifth Avenue, New York, N.Y.
    10022   212-PL9-5959
26555 Evergreen Road, Southfield,
    Mich. 48076   313-355-1900

Campbell-Ewald Co.
3044 W. Grand Blvd., Detroit, Mich.
    48202   313-872-6200

620 Fifth Avenue, New York, N.Y.
10020   212-489-6200
1717 N. Highland Avenue,
Hollywood, Cal. 90028 213-461-3211
1 Maritime Plaza, San Francisco, Cal.
94111   415-989-5556

Campbell-Mithun Inc.
Northstar Center, Minneapolis,
Minn. 55402   612-339-7383
111 E. Wacker Drive, Chicago, Ill.
60601   312-565-3800
200 Fillmore, Denver, Col. 80206 303-399-2962

Compton Advertising Inc.
625 Madison Avenue, New York,
N.Y. 10022   212-PL4-1100
5670 Wilshire Blvd., Suite 2265, Los
Angeles, Cal. 90036 213-937-3610

Cunningham & Walsh Inc.
260 Madison Avenue, New York,
N.Y. 10016   212-683-4900
500 Sansome Street, San Francisco,
Cal. 94111   415-981-7850
One Century Plaza, Los Angeles, Cal.
90067   213-556-1600

Dancer Fitzgerald Sample, Inc.
347 Madison Avenue, New York,
N.Y. 10017   212-679-0600
1010 Battery Street, San Francisco,
Cal. 94111   415-982-8400
5670 Wilshire Blvd., Los Angeles, Cal.
90036   213-937-2710

Del Amo Executive Plaza, 3878
  Carson Street, Torrance, Cal.
  90503   213-540-2554

Daniel & Charles Assocs. Ltd.
  261 Madison Avenue, New York,
  N.Y. 10016   212-MO1-0200

D'Arcy-MacManus & Masius, Inc.
  437 Madison Avenue, New York,
  N.Y. 10022   212-754-2300
  Bloomfield Hills, Mich. 48013   313-MI6-1000
  200 E. Randolph, Chicago, Ill. 60601 312-861-5000
  2900 Turtle Creek Plaza, Dallas, Tex.
  75219   214-522-6630
  1801 Century Park East, Los Angeles,
  Cal. 90067   213-277-2888
  1 Memorial Drive, St. Louis, Mo.
  63102   314-231-6700
  7900 Xerxes Avenue So., Suite 600,
  Bloomington, Minn. 55431   612-831-7900
  433 California Street, San Francisco,
  Cal. 94104   415-391-2750

De Garmo Inc.
  605 Third Avenue, New York, N.Y.
  10016   212-986-2122

Della Femina, Travisano & Partners
  625 Madison Avenue, New York, N.Y.
  10022   212-421-7180
  5900 Wilshire Blvd., Los Angeles, Cal.
  90036   213-937-8540

W. B. Doner & Co.
26711 Northwestern Highway,
Southfield, Mich. 48075   313-354-9700
2305 No. Charles, Baltimore, Md.
21218   301-338-1600

Doremus & Co.
120 Broadway, New York, N.Y.
10005   212-964-0700
660 Madison Avenue, New York, N.Y.
10021   212-758-6617
1701 K Street, N.W., Washington
D.C. 20006   202-296-5527
208 So. LaSalle, Chicago, Ill. 60604   312-CE6-9132
535 Boylston Street, Boston, Mass.
02116   617-261-2560
106 S. 16th St., Philadelphia, Pa.
19102   215-561-0630

Doyle Dane Bernbach, Inc.
437 Madison Avenue, New York, N.Y.
10022   212-826-2000
5900 Wilshire Blvd., Los Angeles,
Cal. 90036   213-937-5100

A. Eicoff & Co.
520 N. Michigan Avenue, Chicago,
Ill. 60611   312-944-2300

Eisaman, Johns & Laws, Inc.
6255 Sunset Blvd., Los Angeles, Cal.
90028   213-469-1234
333 N. Michigan Avenue, Chicago,
Ill. 60601   312-263-3474

964 Third Avenue, New York, N.Y.
10022   212-486-2200
800 Grant Street, Denver, Col. 80203   303-892-7033
20 Providence St., Boston, Mass.
02116   617-426-1025

William Esty Co., Inc.
100 East 42nd Street, New York, N.Y.
10017   212-697-1600

Foote, Cone & Belding
200 Park Avenue, New York, N.Y.
10017   212-973-7000
401 N. Michigan Avenue, Chicago,
Ill. 60611   312-467-9200
2727 W. Sixth St., Los Angeles, Cal.
90057   213-381-6960
55 Francisco, San Francisco, Cal.
94133   415-398-5200

Fox & Assocs. Inc.
Standard Bldg., Cleveland, Ohio.
44113   216-621-8520
137 East 36th Street, New York, N.Y.
10016   212-889-7250
1530 South Sixth St., Minneapolis,
Minn. 55404   612-339-3370

Grey Advertising, Inc.
777 Third Avenue, New York, N.Y.
10017   212-PL1-3500
3435 Wilshire Blvd., Los Angeles,
Cal. 90010   213-380-0530
3003 No. Central Avenue, Phoenix,
Ariz. 85012   602-263-5373

555 California St., San Francisco, Cal.
94104   415-362-0393

Griswold-Eshleman Co.
55 Public Square, Cleveland, Ohio
44113   216-696-3400
655 Madison Avenue, New York, N.Y.
10021   212-838-7100
875 N. Michigan Avenue, Chicago,
Ill. 60611   312-943-6464
Benedum Trees Bldg., 223 Fourth
Avenue, Pittsburgh, Pa. 15222   412-471-5701
Mariemont Executive Bldg., 3814
West Street, Cincinnati, Ohio 45227   513-271-8885

Helfgott, Towne & Silverstein Inc.
1350 Avenue of the Americas, New
York, N.Y. 10019   212-JU2-2100

Hicks & Greist, Inc.
850 Third Avenue, New York, N.Y.
10022   212-421-4200

Kenyon & Eckhardt Advertising Inc.
200 Park Avenue, New York, N.Y.
10017   212-973-2000
10 S. Riverside Plaza, Chicago, Ill.
60606   321-FI6-4020
One Parklane Blvd., Dearborn, Mich.
48126   313-336-6600
111 Pine Street, San Francisco, Cal.
94111   415-981-7270
535 Boylston, Boston, Mass. 02116   617-267-8550

Ketchum, MacLeod & Grove Inc.
  Four Gateway Center, Pittsburgh,
    Pa. 15222   412-261-5100
  90 Park Avenue, New York, N.Y.
    10016   212-983-8000
  3334 Richmond Avenue, Houston,
    Tex. 77006   713-JA3-6811

Lee King & Partners
  360 No. Michigan Avenue, Chicago,
    Ill. 60601   312-645-6600
  1100 Alta Loma Road, Los Angeles,
    Cal. 90069   213-057-2932
  112 Central Park So., New York, N.Y.
    10019   212-245-3334

Leber Katz Partners, Inc.
  767 Fifth Avenue, New York, N.Y. 10022 212-826-3900

Richard K. Manoff, Inc.
  845 Third Avenue, New York, N.Y.
    10022   212-350-9200

Marschalk Co., Inc.
  1345 Avenue of the Americas, New
    York, N.Y. 10019   212-974-7700
  601 Rockwell Avenue, Cleveland,
    Ohio 44114   216-687-8800

Marsteller, Inc.
  866 Third Avenue, New York, N.Y.
    10022   212-752-6500
  One E. Wacker Drive, Chicago, Ill.
    60601   312-329-1100
  One Oliver Plaza, Pittsburgh, Pa.
    15222   412-391-5454

3600 Wilshire Blvd., Los Angeles, Cal.
90005   213-DU8-8600

McCaffrey & McCall, Inc.
575 Lexington Avenue, New York,
N.Y. 10022   212-421-7500

McCann-Erikson, Inc.
485 Lexington Avenue, New York,
N.Y. 10017   212-697-6000
615 Peachtree N.E., Atlanta, Ga.
30308   404-875-0561
Gateway Center, 10 So. Riverside
Plaza, Chicago, Ill. 60606   312-454-7700
Suite 401, 2401 Big Beaver Rd.,
Detroit, Mich. 48084   313-643-4540
800 Bell, Houston, Tex. 77002   713-225-0061
6420 Wilshire Blvd., Los Angeles, Cal.
90048   213-665-9420
900 South West Fifth, Portland, Ore.
97204   503-224-0621
44 Montgomery St., San Francisco,
Cal. 94104   415-981-2262
1001 Fourth Avenue, Seattle, Wash.
98104   206-682-6360

Arthur Meyerhoff Assocs., Inc.
410 No. Michigan Avenue, Chicago,
Ill. 60611   312-DE7-7860

Nadler & Larimer, Inc.
555 Madison Avenue, New York, N.Y.
10022   212-421-6140

Needham, Harper & Steers
909 Third Avenue, New York, N.Y.
10022   212-758-7600
The Chicago Partnership Div., 401 N.
Michigan Avenue, Chicago, Ill.
60611   312-527-3400
Kirkeby Center, 10889 Wilshire Blvd.,
Los Angeles, Cal. 90024   213-478-6525
Suite 2100, Winters Bank Tower,
Dayton, Ohio 45402   513-226-1515
8150 Leesburg Pike, Vienna, Va.
22180   703-790-1090

Norman, Craig & Kummel, Inc.
919 Third Avenue, New York, New
York 10022   212-751-0900

Ogilvy & Mather, Inc.
2 East 48th Street, New York, N.Y.
10017   212-MU8-6100
2600 Two Shell Plaza, Houston, Tex.
77002   713-225-1841
5900 Wilshire Blvd., Los Angeles, Cal.
90036   213-937-7900

Parkson Advertising Agency, Inc.
767 Fifth Avenue, New York, New
York 10022   212-752-3300

Rosenfeld, Sirowitz & Lawson, Inc.
1370 Avenue of the Americas, New
York, N.Y. 10019   212-765-2900
9440 Santa Monica Blvd., Beverly
Hills, Cal. 90210   213-273-7000

Ross Roy, Inc.
  2751 East Jefferson Avenue, Detroit,
    Mich. 48207   313-568-6000
  555 Fifth Avenue, New York, N.Y.
    10017   212-986-6800

SSC&B, Inc.
(Sullivan Stauffer Colwell & Bayles, Inc.)
  One Dag Hammarskjold Plaza, New
    York, N.Y. 10017   212-644-5000
  1800 N. Highland Avenue, Holly-
    wood, Cal. 90028   213-H04-2119

Scali, McCabe, Sloves, Inc.
  800 Third Avenue, New York, N.Y.
    10022   212-421-2050

Tatham-Laird & Kudner
  625 N. Michigan Avenue, Chicago,
    Ill. 60611   312-337-4400
  605 Third Avenue, New York, N.Y.
    10016   212-972-9000

J. Walter Thompson
  420 Lexington Avenue, New York,
    N.Y. 10017   212-MU6-7000
  875 No. Michigan Avenue, Chicago,
    Ill. 60611   312-MO4-6700
  1700 Executive Plaza, Dearborn,
    Mich. 48126   313-336-6900
  10100 Santa Monica Blvd., Los
    Angeles, Cal. 90067   213-553-8383
  Suite 2101, 100 Colony Square,
    Atlanta, Ga. 30361   404-892-2321

1156 15th Street, N.W., Washington, D.C. 20005	202-296-6450
1600 Kapiolani Blvd., Honolulu, Hi. 96814	808-955-4433

Wells, Rich, Greene, Inc.

767 Fifth Avenue, New York, New York 10022	212-PL8-4300
1900 Avenue of the Stars, Los Angeles, Cal. 90067	213-277-3200

Young & Rubicam, Inc.

285 Madison Avenue, New York, N.Y. 10017	212-953-2000
211 W. Fort, Detroit, Mich. 48226	313-963-1345
3435 Wilshire Blvd., Los Angeles, Cal. 90010	213-380-6400
520 B Street, San Diego, Suite 2222, San Diego, Calif. 92101	714-232-7491
3443 N. Central Avenue, Suite 1011, Phoenix, Ariz. 85012	602-264-5558

PUBLIC RELATIONS

Ayer P. R. Service
Div. of N. W. Ayer ABH International

1345 Avenue of the Americas, New York, N.Y. 10019	212-974-7400

(See regional offices under Advertising)

Sydney S. Baron & Company, Inc.
540 Madison Avenue, New York,
   N.Y. 10022   212-751-7100

Bell & Stanton
909 Third Avenue, New York, N.Y.
   10022   212-PL9-4800

Booke & Company
919 Third Avenue, New York, N.Y.
   10022   212-593-8600
300 S. Wacker Drive, Suite 1005,
   Chicago, Ill. 60606   312-922-9393
2811 Wilshire Blvd., Santa Monica,
   Calif. 90403   213-829-4601
4800 San Filipe, Suite 560, Houston,
   Tex. 77027   713-627-0141
1629 K Street, N.W., Suite 800,
   Washington, D.C. 20006   202-833-9638

Bozell & Jacobs P.R. Dept.
One Dag Hammarskjold Plaza, New
   York, N.Y. 10019   212-644-7212
(See regional offices under Adver-
   tising)

Burson-Marsteller
866 Third Avenue, New York, N.Y.
   10022   212-752-8610
One E. Wacker Drive, Chicago, Ill.
   60601   312-329-9292
3600 Wilshire Blvd., Los Angeles,
   Cal. 90005   213-DU6-8776
1776 K St., N.W., Washington, D.C.
   20006   202-883-8550

One Oliver Plaza, Pittsburgh, Pa.
15222   412-391-5454

Carl Byoir & Assocs.
800 Second Avenue, New York, N.Y.
10017   212-986-6100
Suite 1114, 900 Wilshire Blvd., Los
Angeles, Cal. 90017   213-627-6421
100 Bush St., Suite 1801, San
Francisco, Cal. 94104   415-362-6971
Life of Georgia Tower, Suite 1104,
600 W. Peachtree, N.W., Atlanta,
Ga. 30308   404-881-1353
Prudential Plaza, Suite 2430,
Chicago, Ill. 60601   312-332-6300
Buhl Bldg., Rm. 942, Griswold &
Congress Sts., Detroit, Mich.
48226   313-695-3366

Cunningham & Walsh P.R. Dept.
260 Madison Avenue, New York,
N.Y. 10016   212-683-4900
(See regional offices under Advertising)

Darcy Communications
400 Midtown Tower, Rochester,
N.Y. 14604   716-546-6480

Dickson-Basford, Inc.
1301 Avenue of the Americas, New
York, N.Y. 10019   212-956-5200
40 Westminster Street, Providence,
R.I. 02903   401-456-1555

Doremus & Company, P.R. Dept.
120 Broadway, New York, N.Y. 10005   212-964-0700
(See regional offices under Adver-
    tising)

Dudley-Anderson-Yutzy
40 West 57th Street, New York, N.Y.
    10019   212-977-9400
1616 H. Street, N.W., Washington,
    D.C. 20006   202-783-2076
574 Pacific Avenue, San Francisco,
    Cal. 94133   415-981-2261

Daniel J. Edelman, Inc.
221 N. LaSalle Street, Chicago, Ill.
    60601   312-782-9250
711 Third Avenue, New York, N.Y.
    10017   212-557-1020
1730 Pennsylvania Avenue, Wash-
    ington, D.C. 20006   202-782-9400
1901 Avenue of the Stars, Century
    City, Los Angeles, Cal. 90067   213-533-1560
703 Market Street, San Francisco,
    Cal. 94103   415-986-3921

Anthony M. Franco
28 W. Adams Avenue, Detroit, Mich.
    48226   313-692-4510

Albert Frank-Guenther Law
61 Broadway, New York, N.Y. 10006   212-248-5200

Fleishman-Hillard
One Memorial Drive, St. Louis, Mo.
    63102   314-231-1733

Edward Gottlieb & Assocs.
485 Madison Avenue, New York,
    N.Y. 10022   212-421-9220
818 18th St., N.W., Washington,
    D.C. 20006   202-331-7250
3450 Wilshire Blvd., Los Angeles,
    Calif. 90001   213-381-3839

Grey & Davis (Div. of Grey Advertising)
777 Third Avenue, New York, N.Y.
    10017   212-PL2-2200

Harshe-Rotman & Druck, Inc.
108 N. State Street, Chicago, Ill.
    60602   312-346-6868
300 East 44th Street, New York, N.Y.
    10017   212-661-3400
3345 Wilshire Blvd., Los Angeles,
    Calif. 90005   213-385-5271
100 N. Main Street, Memphis, Tenn.
    38103   901-525-2791
One Main Place, Dallas, Tex. 75250 214-748-0802
836 Esperson Bldg., Houston, Tex.
    77002   713-237-9221
1717 K Street, N.W., Washington,
    D.C.   202-296-3049

Hill and Knowlton
633 Third Avenue, New York, N.Y.
    10017   212-697-5600
528 Candler Bldg., 127 Peachtree
    N.E., Atlanta, Ga. 30303   404-523-4606
2001 Bryan Street, Dallas, Tex. 75201 214-651-1761

600 Jefferson Street, Suite 1015,
Houston, Tex. 77002   713-237-9383
1425 K Street, N.W., Washington,
D.C. 20005   202-638-2800
1600 Kapiolani Blvd., Honolulu, Hi.
96814   808-955-1789
5900 Wilshire Blvd., Los Angeles,
Cal. 90036   213-937-7460
44 Montgomery Street, San Francisco,
Cal. 94104   415-392-1810
1143 Washington Bldg., Seattle,
Wash. 98101   206-682-6944

I.C.P.R.
Eighth Floor, 9255 Sunset Blvd.
Los Angeles, Cal. 90069   213-550-8211
Suite 400, 545 Madison Avenue,
New York, N.Y. 10022   212-421-7610

Woody Kepner Assocs.
3361 S.W. Third Avenue, Miami,
Fla. 33145   305-854-4765

Ketchum MacLeod & Grove P.R. Dept.
Four Gateway Center, Pittsburgh,
Pa. 15222   412-261-5100
(See regional offices under Adver-
tising)

Manning Selvage & Lee
666 Fifth Avenue, New York, N.Y.
10019   212-586-2600
1750 Pennsylvania Avenue, N.W.,
Washington, D.C. 20006   202-298-8455

12011 San Vincente Blvd., Los
  Angeles, Cal. 90049 — 213-476-6211
333 No. Michigan Avenue, Chicago,
  Ill. 60601 — 312-726-7890

Robert Marston & Assocs.
645 Madison Avenue, New York, N.Y.
  10022 — 212-LY3-1914

Hank Meyer Assocs., Inc.
2990 Biscayne Blvd., Miami, Fla.
  33137 — 305-576-5700

Padilla and Speer
224 Franklin Avenue West, Minneapolis, Minn. 55404 — 612-871-8900

Rogers & Cowan, Inc.
9665 Wilshire Blvd., Beverly Hills,
  Cal. 90212 — 213-275-4581
415 Madison Avenue, New York,
  N.Y. 10017 — 212-759-6272

The Rowland Co., Inc.
415 Madison Avenue, New York,
  N.Y. 10017 — 212-MU8-1200

Ruder & Finn
110 East 59th Street, New York, N.Y.
  10022 — 212-593-6400
100 Bush Street, San Francisco, Cal.
  94104 — 415-781-2208
9300 Wilshire Blvd., Beverly Hills,
  Cal. 90202 — 213-274-8303
20 N. Wacker Drive, Chicago, Ill.
  60606 — 312-372-4192

1 Turtle Creek Village, Oak Lawn
  Avenue at Blackburn, Dallas, Tex.
    75219   214-521-5672
Capital National Bank Building,
  Houston, Tex. 77002   713-228-8011

The Softness Group
  635 Madison Avenue, New York, N.Y.
    10022   212-PL2-7700

J. Walter Thompson P.R. Dept.
  420 Lexington Avenue, New York,
    N.Y. 10017   212-686-7000
  (See regional offices under Adver-
    tising)

Underwood, Jordan Assocs.
  230 Park Avenue, New York, N.Y.
    10017   212-686-4700
  1115 National Press Bldg., Washing-
    ton, D.C. 20045   202-783-2406

BROADCASTING

American Broadcasting Co.
  1330 Avenue of the Americas, New
    York, N.Y. 10019   212-LT1-7777

CBS Inc.
  51 West 52nd Street, New York,
    N.Y. 10019   212-765-4321

Columbia Pictures Television Division
Colgems Square, Burbank, Cal. 91505   213-843-6000

Cox Broadcasting Corp.
1601 W. Peachtree Street, N.E.,
Atlanta, Ga. 30309   404-897-7000

Fuqua Television, Inc.
1001 Reynolds Street, Augusta, Ga.
30903   404-722-6664

General Electric Broadcasting Co.
1400 Balltown Road, Schenectady,
N.Y. 12309   518-377-2261

Hughs Television Network Inc.
1133 Avenue of the Americas, New
York, N.Y. 10036   212-765-6600

KRON-TV Chronicle Broadcasting Co.
1001 Van Ness Avenue, San Francisco, Cal. 94109   415-441-4444

KXTV, Great Western Broadcasting Corp.
400 Broadway, Sacramento, Cal.
95818   916-441-4041

Kelly Broadcasting Co.
310 10th, Sacramento, Cal. 94813   916-444-7300

Lin Broadcasting Corp.
1370 Avenue of the Americas, New
York, N.Y. 10019   212-765-1902

MCA Inc. MCA TV Div.
445 Park Avenue, New York, N.Y.
10022   212-PL9-7500

Metromedia Inc.
277 Park Avenue, New York, N.Y.
10017   212-682-9100

Mutual Black Network
Mutual Broadcasting System Inc.
World Center Bldg. 918 16th St.,
N.W., Washington, D.C. 20006   202-785-6300

National Broadcasting Co.
30 Rockefeller Plaza, New York, N.Y.
10020   212-617-8300

RKO General Inc.
1440 Broadway, New York, N.Y.
10018   212-764-7000

TVS Television Network
280 Park Avenue, New York, N.Y.
10017   212-697-0660

Taft Broadcasting Co.
1906 Highland, Cincinnati, Ohio
45219   513-721-4114

WGN Continental Broadcasting Co.
2501 Bradley Place, Chicago, Ill.
60618   312-528-2311

WKY Television System Inc.
500 E. Britton Road, Oklahoma City,
Okla. 73114   405-478-1212

Westinghouse Broadcasting Co. Inc.
Group W., 90 Park Avenue, New
York, N.Y. 10016   212-983-6500

MOTION PICTURES

Major Studios and Film Production Houses

Allied Artists Pictures Corp.
  15 Columbus Circle
    New York, N.Y. 10023 — 212-541-9200

American International Pictures
  9033 Wilshire Blvd.
    Beverly Hills, Cal. 90211 — 213-278-8118

Avco Embassy Pictures Corp.
  6601 Romaine Street
    Los Angeles, Cal. 90038 — 213-462-7211
  750 Third Avenue
    New York, N.Y. 10017 — 212-949-8900

Bob Banner Associates, Inc.
  132 South Rodeo Drive
    Beverly Hills, Cal. 90212 — 213-273-6923

Chuck Barris Productions
  1313 North Vine Street
    Los Angeles, Cal. 90028 — 213-469-9080

Brut Productions
  c/o 20th Century Fox
    10210 West Pico Blvd.
      Los Angeles, Cal. 90035 — 213-277-2211

1345 Avenue of the Americas
New York, N.Y. 10019   212-581-3114

Columbia Pictures
The Burbank Studios
1 Columbia Plaza
Burbank, Cal. 91505   213-843-6000
711 Fifth Avenue
New York, N.Y. 10022   212-751-4400

Walt Disney Productions, Inc.
500 South Buena Vista Street
Burbank, Cal. 91521   213-845-3141

Goodson-Todman Productions
6430 Sunset Blvd.
Los Angeles, Cal. 90028   213-461-8211

Metro-Goldwyn Mayer
10202 West Washington Blvd.
Culver City, Cal. 90230   213-836-3000
1350 Avenue of the Americas
New York, N.Y. 10019   212-977-3400

New World Pictures, Inc.
11600 San Vicente Blvd.
Los Angeles, Cal. 90049   213-820-6733

Paramount Pictures Corp.
5451 Marathon Street
Los Angeles, Cal. 90038   213-463-0100

1 Gulf & Western Plaza
New York, N.Y. 10023   212-333-4600

Q. M. Productions
  1041 North Formosa Avenue
    Los Angeles, Cal. 90046   213-851-1234

Radnitz/Mattel, Inc.
  4024 Radford Avenue
    Studio City, Cal. 91604   213-763-8411

Screen Gems
  The Burbank Studio
    300 Colgems Square
      Burbank, Cal. 91522   213-843-7280

Tandem Productions, Inc.
  1901 Avenue of the Stars, Suite 666
    Los Angeles, Cal. 90067   213-553-3600

20th Century Fox Film Corp.
  P.O. Box 900
    Beverly Hills, Cal. 90213   213-277-2211

United Artists Corp.
  10202 West Washington Blvd.
    Culver City, Cal. 90230   213-559-3450
  729 Seventh Avenue
    New York, N.Y. 10019   212-575-3000

Universal Pictures
  Universal City Studios
    Universal City, Cal. 91608   213-985-4321
  445 Park Avenue
    New York, N.Y. 10022   212-759-7500

Warner Bros., Inc.
  4000 Warner Blvd.
    Burbank, Cal. 91522   213-843-6000

75 Rockefeller Plaza
New York, N.Y. 10019 — 212-484-8000

Talent Agencies

Agency for the Performing Arts, Inc.
9000 Sunset Blvd. Suite 315
Los Angeles, Cal. 90069 — 213-273-0744

Bresler, Wolf, Cota & Livingston
190 North Canon Drive
Beverly Hills, Cal. 90210 — 213-278-3200

Chartwell Artists Ltd.
1901 Avenue of the Stars, Suite 670
Los Angeles, Cal. 90067 — 213-553-3600

Chasin-Park-Citron Agency
9255 Sunset Blvd.
Los Angeles, Cal. 90069 — 213-273-7190

Jack Fields & Associates
9255 Sunset Blvd., Suite 1105
Los Angeles, Cal. 90069 — 213-278-1333

Phil Gersh Agency, Inc.
222 North Canon Drive
Beverly Hills, Cal. 90210 — 213-274-6611

International Creative Management
8899 Beverly Blvd.
Los Angeles, Cal. 90048 — 213-550-4000

Kumin-Olenick Agency
400 South Beverly Drive
Beverly Hills, Cal. 90212 — 213-553-8561

The Mishkin Agency
9255 Sunset Blvd.
   Los Angeles, Cal. 90069   213-274-5261

William Morris Agency, Inc.
151 El Camino Drive
   Beverly Hills, Cal. 90212   213-274-7451

Publicity Agencies

Jay Bernstein Public Relations
9110 Sunset Blvd., Suite 250
   Los Angeles, Cal. 90069   213-274-7656

Guttman & Pam Public Relations
404 North Roxbury Drive
   Beverly Hills, Cal. 90210   213-278-6775

Harshe-Rotman & Druck
3345 Wilshire Blvd.
   Los Angeles, Cal. 90010   213-385-5271
400 E. Randolph Street
   Chicago, Ill. 60601   312-527-3730

I.C.P.R. Intercom
9255 Sunset Blvd.
   Los Angeles, Cal. 90069   213-550-8211

Pickwick Public Relations, Inc.
9744 Wilshire Blvd., Suite 209
   Beverly Hills, Cal. 90212   213-273-7344

Rogers & Cowan, Inc.
9665 Wilshire Blvd., Suite 310
   Beverly Hills, Cal. 90212   213-275-4581

Solters/Sabinson/Roskin, Inc.
9255 Sunset Blvd.
    Los Angeles, Cal. 90069   213-275-5303

John Springer Associates
1901 Avenue of the Stars #580
    Los Angeles, Cal. 90067   213-277-3744

Advertising Agency

Diener, Hauser, Greenthal Co., Inc.
9255 Sunset Blvd.
    Los Angeles, Cal. 90069   213-273-3800
25 West 43 Street
    New York, N.Y. 10036   212-564-2100